MW00795838

HIRE BETTER
TEACHERS NOW

HARVARD EDUCATION LETTER
IMPACT SERIES

The *Harvard Education Letter* Impact Series offers an in-depth look at timely topics in education. Individual volumes explore current trends in research, practice, and policy. The series brings many voices into the conversation about issues in contemporary education and considers reforms from the perspective of—and on behalf of—educators in the field.

OTHER BOOKS IN THIS SERIES

Fewer, Clearer, Higher
Robert Rothman

I Used to Think . . . And Now I Think . . .
Edited by Richard F. Elmore

Inside School Turnarounds
Laura Pappano

Something in Common
Robert Rothman

From Data to Action
Edited by Milbrey McLaughlin
and Rebecca A. London

HIRE BETTER TEACHERS NOW

*Using the Science of Selection to Find
the Best Teachers for Your School*

DALE S. ROSE

ANDREW ENGLISH

TREENA GILLESPIE FINNEY

Harvard Education Press
Cambridge, Massachusetts

HARVARD EDUCATION LETTER
IMPACT SERIES

Copyright © 2014 by the President and Fellows of Harvard College

All rights reserved. No part of this publication may be reproduced or transmitted in any form or by any means, electronic or mechanical, including photocopy, recording, or any information storage and retrieval systems, without permission in writing from the publisher.

Library of Congress Control Number 2013951058
Paperback ISBN: 978-1-61250-639-5
Library Edition ISBN: 978-1-61250-640-1

Published by Harvard Education Press,
an imprint of the Harvard Education Publishing Group

Harvard Education Press
8 Story Street
Cambridge, MA 02138

Cover Design: Ciano Design
Cover Images: bubaone/iStock Vectors/Getty Images
The typefaces used in this book are Legacy Serif ITC and Knockout.

CONTENTS

INTRODUCTION

Hire Better Teachers Now offers a research-based approach to help schools and school districts strengthen their overall teaching by improving the way they hire teachers. Our goal in writing this book is to help districts adopt best practices for accurately identifying the *best* teachers available from their existing applicant pool. To do this, it is important to realize that hiring is an entirely practical decision. That is, district-level hiring managers (and principals within individual schools) should recognize that hiring is a multiple-choice test: the right choice is always *the best answer from the available options*, even if an imaginary other option would be ideal. To this end, this book can be used as a detailed study guide for the test districts face when hiring new faculty. Step by step, we detail how school districts can leverage research-based tools to identify which of the imperfect choices they face is best qualified.

By choosing the best teachers, schools have a chance to radically improve educational outcomes for their students. Student outcomes will improve by making better hiring decisions, and the best hiring decisions will result when districts leverage the well-researched science behind effective hiring practices.

Of course, we realize that school districts across the country are faced with a myriad of challenges when considering how to enhance their hiring processes. A one-size-fits-all approach to hiring teachers will likely fail for many districts. Even some of the most successful teacher training and recruitment programs have demonstrated mixed results with respect to teacher retention after job placements have been made. Instead of introducing a single hiring solution for all schools to adopt uniformly, we introduce a set of recommendations for improving the hiring process with clear, scientifically grounded guidance on how to optimize each hiring tool to suit a school's or district's unique characteristics, available resources, and day-to-day challenges.

Whether you work at a newly formed charter school that needs to hire a new faculty or you represent a large district that has a sophisticated hiring process honed over many years, this book provides you with ways to level-up the quality of your new hires. The methods we describe are grounded in a very mature and well-tested science of how to make good hiring decisions. We know these tools can improve any district's hiring because we've read the research and seen it work in schools. We've talked to teachers and principals about what works and what doesn't, and we've done the research which proves that these methods get results.

In our work helping schools and other organizations improve their hiring practices, we emphasize making changes that fit the school's unique environment. These changes can be big or small, but even small improvements make an impact when scientifically proven methods are used instead of ad hoc or informal processes. While the effort to build and research hiring systems can be large, schools can get a great deal out of something as simple as a well-designed training program for interviewers. Regardless of whether you build an entire suite of well-researched tools or just make small, incremental improvements, if you can improve your hiring processes, you will hire better teachers, which will result in better outcomes for your students. And, after all, isn't that what the best of our educational institutions are all about?

Our recommendations are not based on our opinions and experience alone. Nor are they based on only our research. Throughout the book, we point to a significant body of peer-reviewed research with the hope that this level of detail will help convey to you, our reader (and the skeptics you may work with), the value of and potential for the methods we suggest. And if the research we cite in the first eight chapters isn't enough for a district to believe that the results will improve, in chapter 9 we describe methods a district can use to document its own successes and thereby find ways to improve even more.

Too few districts using research-based tools has a negative impact on aggregate teacher quality nationally and is likely a significant contributor to poor student outcomes. Of course, districts do not *want* to make poor decisions when hiring teachers; it's just that they are often faced with difficult choices and are poorly equipped to choose among the candidates. Hiring is necessarily pragmatic; and with teacher hiring this is even more salient. It is estimated that as many as 62 percent of teachers are hired within a month of the start date. Hence, in practice, schools are rarely in a position to choose among a large number of clearly qualified candidates. Using the methods we propose, districts will be able to choose the *best available* candidate. Thus, districts that have a dearth of applicants will be able to avoid hiring the truly low performing teachers, and districts that have a large pool of qualified candidates will be able to reliably differentiate the great teachers from the good teachers.

3

Consider the following scenario: You are the human resources manager of a school district, and three weeks before the fall semester a seventh grade pre-algebra teacher informs you that she has accepted a position elsewhere. This is inappropriate, unprofessional, and inconvenient—but regardless of how much you dislike the situation, you need to fill the position quickly. After searching around for a bit and advertising the job, you manage to attract three applicants for the opening. Based on a quick review of their resumes, you see that Applicant 1 has only taught high school students in calculus, chemistry, and geometry; Applicant 2 has been teaching basic math to sixth and seventh grade students at a nearby middle school in the same district; and Applicant 3 has never taught in the schools but has been a trainer in programming languages for several nearby companies and has an advanced degree in math. The principal spent an hour talking with each candidate. Applicant 3 impressed her the most. This candidate was very professional but also friendly and enthusiastic. Applicant 2 also impressed her. This candidate was very familiar with the age group and seemed like he would fit well in the school. Applicant 1, however, seemed a bit introverted and nervous and was overeager for the job. So who should you hire?

Of course, none of these candidates is the perfect choice, and yet school districts nationwide face this kind of choice every year. Sadly, too often the district lets the principal decide based on nothing more than information like what's presented above. The odds of making the right choice based on the available information is about 1 in 3—in other words, pick a name out of a hat. Yet, an HR manager with a set of validated screening tools could invest as little as five hours of staff time on all the candidates and improve the odds of making the right hire.

A valid interview and job simulation exercise could easily reveal that Applicant 3 has no ability to organize or adjust a lesson plan, that Applicant 2 doesn't understand algebra well enough to teach it, and that Applicant 1 not only knows the material but also excels at handling split classrooms, where some students struggle and others are bored by the same material (a common problem in pre-algebra).

Whereas many principals feel they have a great instinct for hiring, evidence shows otherwise. All people (even the most brilliant principals!) are prone to bias, can overlook facts, and can be easily swayed by factors not relevant to a job (such as physical attractiveness, extroversion, and credentials that look impressive but don't actually predict performance). With the right tools and a small investment of time, districts can guarantee themselves significantly better teachers over the long run. Consider the example above. Applicants 2 and 3 are the mostly likely to be chosen based on the principal's impressions. For the district, however, hiring Applicant 2 simply moves the problem from one school to the next. And Applicant 3 may be impressive in an interview, but that doesn't mean he can teach students. Meanwhile, Applicant 1 is overlooked simply because he was a little nervous during the interview, despite the fact that this does not correlate with teaching outcomes.

WHO SHOULD READ THIS BOOK?

District administrators and HR personnel will benefit the most from reading this book and using it in an effort to address their continued frustration with the highly varied and (sometimes) ineffectual hiring methods currently in use. A common complaint among district administrators and HR personnel is that while some principals seem good at hiring, others do not, and no one uses the same approach (which creates a significant legal risk and results in many bad hires every year). This book can be used by district staff to audit existing systems and identify specific elements to level-up or as a guide for developing a hiring system from the ground up.

The book will also be valuable for any charter school or district, as these bodies will need to develop some sort of hiring process—so why not start with a process that is reliable and valid? Additionally, any school that anticipates significant growth or regularly hires large numbers of teachers due to natural attrition should find our hiring funnel concept very useful.

Principals who would like to improve hiring in their own school (either in concert with or independent of district requirements) will find many small tips for and practical insights into how they can become better at hiring teachers. With more than 80 percent of teachers interviewed by principals, it is clear that these administrators are an important component of the hiring process, and, with their institutional focus, the best among them should be interested in improving.

With this in mind, graduate programs in education administration could use all or parts of the book to help students explore one of the most critical processes for building excellence into schools. It is very hard to excel in any organization if you don't have a way to accurately identify the best members to achieve your goals. As such, the management and administration component of graduate curricula could benefit from some well-grounded methods for identifying the best faculty.

The techniques we describe will be valuable to researchers in the field of education who are studying effective teaching and trying to demonstrate that one teaching method, skill set, or behavior is superior to others. We do not advocate for a particular set of teaching skills, or even a specific set of outcomes to measure. Instead, we provide a scientifically proven way to evaluate which tools most accurately predict intended outcomes. As such, any set of outcomes (e.g., test scores, graduation rates, or employment level of graduates) and predictors (hiring tools) can be plugged into our methods. While we cannot guarantee that a particular hiring tool will predict a particular outcome, we can guarantee that if researchers use the methods we describe, they will have clear and compelling evidence about how well their chosen tools predict their chosen outcomes.

HOW TO READ THIS BOOK

Hire Better Teachers Now gives readers comprehensive knowledge about how to build and evaluate selection systems to predict specific outcomes. We include elements of the history and core concepts behind the science of hiring best practices (chapters 1 and 3); a detailed discussion about how to identify what good teaching means in your school setting (chapter 2); detailed discussion, with examples, about how to build high-quality teacher screening tools (chapters 4–8); guidance for how to level-up hiring processes at any school suited to any budget (chapter 9); and considerations of practical issues facing schools when trying to use sophisticated hiring systems (chapter 10).

Each chapter stands as a valuable tool in its own right. For example, a school trying to improve its interview process could leverage insights from chapter 5, which delves deeply into what makes a highly effective interview. After reading chapter 5, it may help to also explore the concepts of validity and reliability in chapter 3 and to at least skim elements of chapter 8, to see how to compare applicants, and chapter 9, where we explore ways to tailor your efforts to fit your budget.

The content of this book is supported by peer-reviewed scientific evidence. Any chapter can be a valuable resource for finding the latest (and longest-standing) research to support best practices in hiring, with an emphasis on the tools we cover: application forms (chapter 4), interviews (chapter 5), work samples (chapter 6), and teaching observations (chapter 7).

While we introduce here a comprehensive set of tools and a process that can help districts effectively identify the best teacher candidates, we do not cover all considerations that may be needed to actually place a teacher in the job. For instance, we intentionally exclude discussions of background screening, finger printing, or reference checking. While all of these things are good to do, none of them helps districts hire better teachers; they do, however, prevent districts from hiring absurdly bad teachers, and most of these steps are mandated by law (and these laws differ by state, region, and even district). We also do not mention anything about recruitment, which, when done well, can also have an extraordinary influence (good and bad) on the quality of teachers hired.

Hire Better Teachers Now can certainly be used as a starting point. But it can also be used as a means of auditing an existing hiring process. If your hiring process stands up well to the recommendations we provide, then congratulations, you've got a world-class hiring process. It wouldn't surprise us, however, if even the most sophisticated of schools find at least some help in these pages for improving on how they are currently selecting teachers.

1

LEARNING FROM
SELECTION RESEARCH

Like any hiring decision, choosing which teachers to hire is an effort to accurately predict each individual's likelihood of success on the job. Just as individual teachers greatly impact each student's success, so too does each teacher greatly impact the success of a school and the success of a school district. It is reasonable to suggest, then, that one of the single greatest opportunities to improve educational outcomes at any school or school district is to make better hiring decisions. One principal we spoke with made this point quite bluntly. He was just finishing a twenty-five-year career leading a wildly successful high school, and, when asked about his secret to success, he flatly stated, "I hired great teachers, and on the few occasions when I made mistakes, I faced the music and sent them packing." Needless to say, not all schools have this experience.

As any principal or school administrator knows, hiring great teachers is no easy task. While teacher hiring decisions have a

huge impact on the success or failure of a school, these decisions are made under some of the most challenging of circumstances. While some one-off hiring decisions are made during
the year or at the last minute, most districts hire large numbers
of teachers during the spring by screening batches of applicants. Time is of the essence, and resources are scarce. Further
complicating the situation is the fact that subject matter makes
job-candidate fit unbalanced across the system. Districts are
notoriously overwhelmed with applicants for positions teaching the humanities, and yet they may only have two applicants
for each opening in math or science. Even worse, applicants
may be available in math or science but at the wrong grade
level. A common discussion between principals and district HR
managers is whether a teacher with sixth grade math experience could teach a tenth grade geometry class.

When schools hire teachers, they do not have the luxury of
waiting for the perfect candidates. Unlike other organizations,
schools cannot just double-up their effort or have a manager
fill a job for a month or two while continuing to look for stronger candidates. Students will arrive ready to learn, and when
they do, a competent teacher needs to be in the classroom. So,
with time tight, resources scarce, and nothing more than our
children's future is at stake, the pressure is on. And while everyone involved is trying to choose the *best* fit, it is essential to
remember that they are also simply trying to hire someone to
fill the job. Given this, it is perhaps useful to recognize that the
hiring process for any job is a very practical exercise. Every hiring decision comes down to making the best choice among the
available alternatives.

For school districts that have not taken a hard look at how
they hire, there may not be a single program, project, or system-

wide initiative that could make a bigger difference in school success than improving their hiring process. For those districts that have well-established hiring processes, procedures, and policies in place, it may be useful to take a closer look at each step in the process and consider how well those procedures fit within the science of hiring. Indeed, it may be worth gathering specific evidence to confirm assumptions that the process works well. And for any districts that are still hiring teachers by relying on principals with the mantra, "Give me five minutes and I can find the good ones," the rest of this book will provide some great tools for improving student outcomes.

HIRING PLUMBERS VERSUS HIRING TEACHERS

Whether hiring a plumber or hiring a teacher, knowing who will be the best employee requires accurate information about which candidate has the best skill set, the best attitude, and the best knowledge in their domain. Of course, hiring teachers is a lot trickier than hiring plumbers, if only because school districts often hire large numbers of new teachers at about the same time every year. Depending on the labor market, a typical school may get as many as fifty applications for a single teaching spot. For a school that will hire two dozen new teachers, it could be looking at more than a thousand applicants. While this situation presents an excellent opportunity for schools to add top new talent to their teaching ranks, the risk of hiring poorly has significant negative long-term consequences for the school and the students it serves. So, how should schools choose the best teachers?

The simple truth is that most schools don't choose the best teachers as often as they would like. When hiring teachers, many districts use outdated personnel selection methods that are not supported by the research and often result in far more hiring mistakes than necessary. Candidates typically complete an application (resume, references, etc.), undergo a brief pre-screening with HR, and then have an unstructured interview with the principal. In each of these steps, initial impressions, job tenure, affiliations (which schools attended, certifications, professional association, etc.), and personal connections (referrals, known associates, friends, etc.) are given considerable weight in the hiring decision. It often surprises principals to learn that all of these sources of information have shown only very weak correlations with job performance.[1] As a result, schools make many hiring decisions on the basis of factors unrelated to successful teaching.

Of course, even with a typical informal hiring process, not all hiring decisions will be bad. Even in selecting teachers at random, some good hires make it through along with the average and poor performers. This "method" can actually work reasonably well when you are hiring plumbers. One can hire a plumber, put them on the job, and see how they do. If the faucets they fix still leak or the hot water doesn't get hot, the evidence of their failure is immediate and objective. With teachers, however, hiring a wide range of performers poses some significant problems. Indeed, forty-three states use a probationary period before giving a teacher tenure status.[2] While this sounds good in theory, to improve teacher quality, districts need to be far more selective about which teachers are retained after their initial pretenure probationary period, because (depending on the labor contract) once they have passed through probation, districts may not be able to screen teachers out based on performance. Part of the challenge with this is that a teacher's performance is often difficult to determine as quickly or as precisely as a plumber's performance. Indeed, probationary periods are no guarantee, unless districts have a rigorous assessment process to ensure that only the best teachers are retained past probation. Perhaps the bigger challenge to screening out probationary teachers is the obstacle presented by teacher unions, which are strongly motivated to retain members and will likely resist any such staffing changes.

If districts do not use probationary periods to identify the best teachers, they will be well served to choose wisely at the start. It is also useful to consider the difficulty of removing teachers and the extraordinary expense required to remedy a poor performing teacher.[3] In short, districts are far better off hiring better teachers to start with rather than trying to "fix" teachers who shouldn't have been hired in the first place.

Instead of investing heavily in trying to evaluate, remediate, and develop teachers who are failing, districts could save significant sums of money and drastically improve the district-wide quality level of instruction if they use rigorous scientific methods to ensure that quality teachers are hired in the first place. Evidence shows that many applicants for teaching positions are highly unlikely to succeed as teachers. For instance, the Houston Independent School District (HISD) recently tried to hire about 1,200 new teachers to fill positions vacant due to turnover. They found that 30 percent of new teacher applicants for elementary school teaching positions failed to pass a required fifth grade math test.[4] Indeed, after implementing a more rigorous hiring system, including the use of structured interviews, HISD found that only 12 percent of candidates were qualified. Districts that are not using more advanced screening protocols like this are likely hiring many of the 88 percent that

HISD was able to screen out. And once these poor-performing teachers are hired, extensive, long-term investment in professional development is the only way to remedy the situation.

HISTORY OF SELECTION RESEARCH

There is a very mature research base documenting methods for accurately predicting success in nearly every job. Ironically, one of the conclusions from this research is that some of the same methods used for hiring plumbers can also be used for hiring teachers. Clearly, the knowledge base is different, but in both cases a well-executed, structured interview will produce better hiring decisions than an unstructured interview or even a review of work history.

The first known tests of person-job fit were conducted in China as early as 605 C.E., where the Imperial Examination was used to screen applicants to administrative positions within the government. While the exam was modified frequently across empires, China's present-day Civil Service Exam is an indirect descendant of the original Imperial Examination.[5] China uses standardized testing to identify the best-qualified candidates for civil service positions. With over a million applicants to the most-sought-after jobs, the test had only a 1.28 percent acceptance rate in 2009.[6]

In the United States, the use of standardized testing during hiring began in the early twentieth century, but it wasn't until World War II that the science of selection emerged. During the war, the U.S. Army tasked industrial psychologists with building tests to classify recruits into jobs they were best suited for. With hundreds of thousands of new recruits to screen and place in short order, the military quickly realized that accuracy in placement could have a significant impact on the outcome of the war. For instance, tests were devised to assess mechanical ability, typing skill, and mental acuity. High scores on these tests helped ensure that clerks could type, auto mechanics had adequate strength and dexterity, and intelligence officers were in fact intelligent.

While these tests were important for job placement during the war, the success of this large-scale testing program hinged not only on creating the tests but on the research conducted to ensure the accuracy of prediction. The teams building these tests conducted research to identify how many people the test identified as "passing" actually succeeded on the job as predicted. For example, if 10,000 new recruits were tested on typing ability, and 1,000 of them "passed," how many of these 1,000 would actually be good at a clerical job? Further, how many of the 9,000 who didn't pass would have been effective in a clerical job? The army recognized that it would have a much more effective clerical staff if the tests could aid in making more correct decisions, both in terms of passing and failing scores.

The method devised for assessing test accuracy was to collect test scores from a statistically reliable sample and then correlate them with measures of job performance. While behavioral scientists have conducted thousands of studies to refine these techniques over the years, the fundamental approach remains: first, test a pool of candidates on job-related constructs (typing speed/accuracy) and then correlate test scores with job performance (supervisor ratings of competency in a clerical job). The stronger the correlation, the better the test will predict performance for future applicants.

While the testing program of the 1940s was successful in many ways and provided many lessons about the science of selection, it wasn't until corporations saw the value of testing that these methods became widespread. Following the passage of the Civil Rights Act of 1964, a number of legal cases during the 1970s were decided against employers (e.g., *Griggs v. Duke Power*, 1971), asserting that that all hiring decisions needed to be based solely on bona fide occupational requirements. That is, nonbiased hiring had to be based on factors that actually predict job performance. With the very real threat of costly civil rights lawsuits looming, employers invested heavily for several decades in perfecting the methods of hiring by clearly defining the job-related knowledge, skills, and abilities for each job and building "tests" that could measure those characteristics. We use *test* somewhat loosely here. For our purposes, a test would be any assessment used to determine a candidate's suitability for a job. This could include interviews, application blanks, a written exam, or even a casual review of a resume. Following guidance from the courts, however, employers couldn't stop at just building a good test; they had to prove that the tests were accurate. Following this effort, there was a significant increase in research that documented the effectiveness of research-based methods for screening applicants.[7] Today, nearly all public companies regularly conduct rigorous research to prove that the methods they use to screen applicants predict job performance accurately and don't result in bias against any legally protected groups.

While there is little doubt that corporations were dragged into the employment testing business by the courts, it is the organizations' accountants' and investors' interests that have maintained and even expanded the use of testing. One of the early insights companies made in conducting all of this research was the lesson the army had learned decades before. Namely, by decreasing hiring mistakes, you end up hiring better typists, which will result in a more effective clerical unit. It turns out that this basic rule translates into significant benefit for organizations that have a vested interest in being more effective and efficient.

Over the last two decades, our own research has shown that testing translated into better service in restaurants, greater patient satisfaction in hospitals, decreased voluntary turnover in retail settings, more accurate Medicare reimbursements at a health management organization, and more effective managers at a financial services institution. Not surprisingly, when we turned our attention to schools, we also found that well-built screening tools can also predict success for teachers.[8] So, whether hiring teachers or hiring plumbers, there are some proven methods that will lead to better choices. The exact information gathered may differ, but the way the information is gathered, scored, and interpreted is often much the same.

BETTER TEACHERS MAKE BETTER SCHOOLS

While carefully conducted testing of applicants does result in more effective employees across all jobs, not all testing methods are created equal. And, of course, not all organizations have taken the time to examine job effectiveness, build tests to suit each job, and then conduct research to prove the accuracy of decisions made using test results.

While many principals and HR managers pride themselves on being good judges of character or being skilled at interviewing candidates, research shows that the idea of being an "expert interviewer" is more myth than reality. For example, a review of eighty-five studies examining the effects of interviewing methods found that typical interviews that rely on interviewer ability correlate about .20 with job performance (thus predicting only about 4 percent of variance in performance on the job).[9] Yet, structured interviews that rely on standardized procedures (i.e., preset questions and clear scoring benchmarks) were found to correlate .57 with job performance (accounting for over 32 percent of variance in job performance).

For every student in every classroom, making even one better hiring decision is a worthwhile venture. While each student's learning is important, the true benefits of using best practices in hiring are evident when looking at the potential impact across an entire district. Even during lean years, large districts may hire 500 to 1,000 new teachers due solely to retirements and resignations. At this scale, the benefits of research-based hiring methods become very apparent. If one hiring method results in 60 percent "good hires" and another method results in a 40 percent success rate, a district hiring 1,000 new teachers stands to gain 200 more quality teachers by using the better method. In turn, these 200 will likely produce greater student outcomes (e.g., learning, graduation rates, behavior, etc.). They may also be more likely to stay employed, thus reducing the district's turnover costs, requiring less training and development resources, and being less likely to burden the district through disciplinary actions or other remedial efforts required of poor performing teachers.

So, is it possible to get such large districtwide gains by using best practices in hiring? Not only is it possible, but, by conducting the follow up research, it is possible to quantify the effects. At one school district, we used rigorously designed screening tools that resulted in a test-to-performance correlation (validity coefficient) of R = .51 (accounting for 26 percent of the variance in teacher performance). *Validity coefficient* refers to a correlation between a screening tool and job performance. Correlations range from 0 to 1.0. In practice, validity coefficients range from weak (.15) to moderate (.30) to strong (.50).[10] Consider a typical screening process that includes an informal prescreen followed by an unstructured group interview and then an unstructured principal interview. Such a screening process might result in a validity coefficient of R = .15. Using our methods, hiring decisions are thirteen times more accurate (26 percent of variance versus 2 percent of variance accounted for) than decisions made using the typical process.

In practical terms, correlations in the low teens tend to be considered fairly poor predictors of performance, and anything above a .30 can be considered a valuable tool to improve hiring (see chapter 3 for more detail on validity coefficients). For example, using the typical selection methods (with a validity coefficient of .15), a district screens 100 teachers in order to hire 30 (selection rate of 30 percent). Out of these 100 applicants, half are actually effective teachers (base rate of 50 percent) and half are poor performers. If the district uses its typical tool (with a validity coefficient of .15), it is likely to make the correct hiring decision (rejecting poor performers *and* selecting good ones) for only about 17 of the 30 teachers it hires. If the district uses the more effective methods that we propose (with a validity coefficient of .51), then about 23 of the 30 teachers hired will be effective. While a difference of six teachers might not sound like a lot initially, consider the difference in academic outcomes for the students of those six good teachers as compared to the outcomes if they had six poor performing teachers. And in expanding the scope to include more than 1,000 new hires, the difference in outcomes between using typical hiring processes versus research-based tools becomes even more substantial.

Hiring Better Teachers Improves Educational Outcomes

Teachers matter. Most anyone in the field of education will agree that a good teacher can make a huge difference in learning outcomes for students. But how much of a difference do teachers make? If we hire a good teacher, how much better outcomes can we expect compared to hiring a mediocre teacher? This consideration is important when hiring because it can influence decisions about how much effort to put into hiring decisions. For example, selecting astronauts is a very expensive and elaborate process. Part of the reason for these large investments is that bad hiring decisions are very expensive when it comes to space travel. Poor performance among astronauts can cause the loss of life and very expensive equipment, not to mention result in the wasted expense of operating failed space missions from Earth.

While teaching doesn't carry quite the expense or risk that space travel does, performance differences for teachers have significant impact on important outcomes. Research has demonstrated that "a good teacher will get a gain [in student achievement] of 1.5 grade level equivalents while a bad teacher will get 0.5 year for a single academic year."[11] Thus, while the best results come from hiring only great teachers, a district could benefit immensely by simply hiring more good (as well as more great) teachers and fewer weak teachers.

Not surprisingly, better teachers get better results with students. Based on this premise, every school district in the country pours significant resources into developing their faculty for just this purpose. Yet, despite this effort, there remain many struggling teachers (with predictable results on student outcomes). In fact, developing better teachers may not be the best use of these resources unless a valid screening process is put into place. If better teachers were hired to start with, this would decrease pressure on scarce development resources and would mean that teachers who will benefit from development can get the support they need.

Hire Versus Fire

One of the clearest advantages to hiring better teachers is that doing so reduces the need to fire poor performing teachers. While firing any employee should be an act of last resort, the fact is that in any job some employees simply do not perform at a standard needed to accomplish the goals of the organization. Indeed, just as high performing teachers can help a district excel, poor performing teachers can drag down overall educational quality. By one researcher's estimates, removing the bottom 6–10 percent of teachers nationally based on performance would lead to a gain in student achievement that would move the United States from being ranked twenty-ninth globally to seventh.[12] Such a move would allow the United States to just about compete with Canada.

Of course, no one is suggesting that large swaths of teachers be suddenly removed from service. Firing poor performing teachers is unusually difficult, time consuming, and costly. For instance, by closely following the procedure outlined in the employment contract, there are no fewer than twenty-seven steps required to remove teachers in the Chicago Public Schools, and the process is expected to last two to five years. In New York, it is estimated to cost approximately $250,000 to fire just a single teacher, which likely explains why in 2007 only ten of the city's 55,000 teachers were fired.[13] Such circumstances are common in school districts and result in a remarkably stable workforce. The effects of such stability can be staggering in financial

21

terms. Consider that in 2012, after the New York City district announced it had *fixed* the problem, more than 200 "educators accused of breaking rules, abusing kids . . . will be paid a stunning $22 million by [the] city for doing absolutely nothing" while sitting in reassignment centers.[14]

Instead of looking at firing the bottom 6–10 percent of teachers based on performance, using better hiring tools can prevent these teachers from being hired in the first place. In other words, rather than deselecting teachers, as some research suggested, a far more palatable and perhaps equitable solution is to simply select the best teachers to start with.[15] Using research-based methods, districts can screen out poor performers, which will decrease hiring mistakes, and increase the number of highly talented teachers.

Investing for the Future

Even in the best of times, budgets are tight for schools. Human resources efforts such as hiring, recruiting, and training all represent significant portions of every district's operational budget. The research and development efforts required to significantly upgrade the effectiveness of a hiring process can involve a considerable up-front investment. The costs of these efforts will range widely depending on the current state of the hiring system, the depth of research used (e.g., job analysis only or also doing validation research), and the number of new tools developed. It is reasonable to assume that a district could develop a simple but valid screening tool with a budget of $25,000. Yet, there is almost no limit to what can be done when sophisticated research is involved. We have seen highly elaborate processes with extensive research and training exceed $250,000, so being clear up front about priorities and scope is important. Districts must keep in mind, however, that these are not ongoing operational expenses. They are generally one-time investments that can continue adding value for a decade or more. There are also ways to make small adjustments that can make a big difference before larger efforts can be undertaken. Indeed, there are many steps districts can take that require little or no investment beyond staff time (see chapter 9). Regardless of the level of investment, the returns from improvements in hiring processes can be quite significant. Research-based hiring represents a long-term investment in high-quality education. These tools offer a proven method for enhancing teaching quality in schools, and well after they are implemented, these tools will continue to pay dividends in the form of improved educational outcomes.

SUMMARY

The science behind best practices in hiring has a long history, with many successes, and a literature rich with conclusions about what methods result in the best hiring decisions. While it is clear that better teachers get better results with students, many schools have yet to take steps to ensure that they choose the best available teachers when hiring. Among those districts that already use these methods, many may not have taken the extra step to conduct their own research program to ensure reliability and validity in the current population. For any district serious about improving teacher quality, a clear first step is to invest in building and consistently using rigorously researched screening tools.

2

DETERMINING WHAT
MAKES AN EFFECTIVE TEACHER
IN YOUR SCHOOL

All improvements to hiring processes start by analyzing what makes an effective teacher, with some attention to fit with a particular school. For many reasons, this is not an easy job. The definition of effective teaching is hazy, and researchers concede that there "remains a debate about what constitutes an effective teacher."[1] We're reminded of Supreme Court Justice Potter Stewart's "I know it when I see it" comment in his opinion in *Jacobellis v. Ohio* (1964), when he was struggling to describe obscenity. We might know effective teaching when we see it, but we wrestle with how to define it in behavioral terms.

In a sense, you might think about effective teaching as an abstract work of art: it looks different from various angles. While the academic program graduating teachers focuses on certain criteria (e.g., minimum grade point averages), the teacher values certain, and sometimes different, behaviors as important for her success (e.g., knowledge of current events in her field), and her coworkers focus on other behaviors in describing her effectiveness (e.g., meeting deadlines for committee work) and the principal still others (e.g., willingness to volunteer to help the school, builds relationships with parents). Of course, these lists are not mutually exclusive; that is, subject matter knowledge might be important from all perspectives, but it's helpful to consider research that documents these perspectives.

Professors at the University of Nebraska at Kearney identified eight components in which teacher candidates must demonstrate proficiency to complete their student teaching.[2] These areas include:

- Knowledge of objectives and state standards
- Knowledge of assessment and evaluation
- Knowledge of self-reflection and self-assessment
- Knowledge of instructional planning
- Knowledge of instructional methods
- Knowledge of professional responsibility
- Knowledge of classroom management
- Knowledge of collaboration with other teachers

They found that most stakeholders (e.g., hiring officials, cooperating and supervising teachers) considered these components essential or of a high priority in the hiring process of first-year teachers. In addition to these professional components, they found that selection committees also considered personal qualities (e.g., enthusiasm, communication skills) in making decisions. However, different stakeholders ranked professional and personal characteristics in different orders, suggesting that teachers, principals, and even the candidates themselves might have different ideas of what is essential or important to teaching effectiveness. As a result of their analyses, the researchers indicate that hiring officials desire candidates who are academically prepared and who are passionate about teaching, who have initiative, who can reflect on their methods, who can adjust their teaching philosophy, and who can develop positive relationships with others, including students.

Research centered on principals' perspectives echoes these findings. In one study of principals, the researcher documented teacher screening and selection practices to determine which criteria principals feel are the most important in hiring teachers.[3] Although academic proficiency has been found to be important to effectiveness, it was considered the least important of the criteria used by administrators to hire teachers. In the sample of twenty-eight principals, for example, 32 percent considered "teaching portfolio quality" as an important or very important hiring criterion, and only 22 percent considered college grade point average as important or very important. However, principals ranked as top criteria in hiring: educational background (96 percent) and work experience (96 percent) as listed on the application or resume, the quality of the writing in the resume (86 percent) and the cover letter (82 percent), and student teaching practicum reports (79 percent). Rather than academic proficiency, the principals focused on the academic program candidates attended, whether or not candidates were experienced, and their written communication skills.

Similarly, other research has established that principals generally use professional attributes examined through letters of references, resumes, teaching experience, and grade point average to make the initial cut.[4] They then examine, during the face-to-face interview, the candidates' personal attributes, such as appearance, communication skills, and enthusiasm. Thus, principals tend to define the qualifications of the teacher as professional and personal, with the professional qualifications helping the candidates gain entry to the selection system. Additionally, some have noted that professional qualifications, such as grade point average, are straightforward and objective measures, while personal characteristics, such as enthusiasm, are more nebulous to define and could be less defensible as criteria if a rejected candidate challenges the selection process.[5]

For example, researchers have examined to what extent school districts or administrators alter their teacher selection practices when faced with policies designed to improve teacher quality.[6] Using a Florida sample of principals and administrators, they found that the administrators "bridged," or complied with policy messages for improving teacher quality, by focusing first on professional qualifications of candidates. They then "buffered" the mandated policy and negotiated the policies to fit their own goals beyond the mandated policy by considering fit characteristics, such as personality and diversity. In the study, principals differed in how strongly they considered professional qualifications or personal characteristics in teacher selection. Professional-focused principals evaluated characteristics consistent with ideas of teacher quality (e.g., academic background, experience), while personality-focused principals looked for caring, enthusiasm, and similar characteristics. Most principals had a personality/professional mixed focus. Thus, although the principals complied with mandated teacher quality policy, they also considered other areas as important for teacher quality and took those into consideration when making hiring decisions. Many principals explained that they considered other values important that transcended the state and federal mandates; in particular, they valued outcomes such as principal autonomy in decision making and cultivating a racially diverse faculty and felt that these issues should be considered, although they are not included in teacher certification or other quality measures. Most of the principals surveyed indicated that they prefer candidates who have professional characteristics that are consistent with accountability goals, such as teaching skills and subject matter knowledge. This is encouraging, given that certification and a major in the teaching field are more powerful predictors of student achievement than are education levels (e.g., master's degree).[7] Similarly, in math classes, research has found no effect for a master's degree or even years of experience in predicting student learning; however, pedagogy coursework outside math did predict student achievement in math.[8]

Some research has noted the increasing importance of teacher values as predicting teaching success. For example, some studies contend that effective teachers have value systems that meld well with the goals of education, such as valuing patience and caring or being committed to helping others learn. To evaluate this contention, researchers examined a commercially available instrument that assesses values and attitudes and is used in selection.[9] They found a relatively modest correlation (.28 to .32) between performance on this assessment and teacher quality. The authors of the study contend that ideal beliefs, attitudes, and values may be different for elementary, middle, or high school, and they found a stronger correlation for secondary school teachers than for elementary teachers. One difficulty pointed out is that teacher selection devices assess a teacher's espoused theory but do not necessarily predict how teachers will act or what they will actually do in the classroom. It's important to note that how "effectiveness" is defined influences the strength of the relationship. The scores were more predictive of ratings within the school (e.g., principals) than for external assessment of effectiveness (e.g., external observers).[10] Again, the definition of effectiveness is in the eye of the beholder.

One challenge in defining effective teaching behaviors is that even members of one source (e.g., principals) disagree on what qualities should be emphasized. For example, a study of school administrators found that they preferred different characteristics of teachers and used different selection tools to measure these characteristics.[11] In addition, principals "mix and match" the characteristics of the teachers to fill voids in diversity and skill and to make sure that teachers fit into the norms and values of the school. The study's authors noted that "as long as there is ambiguity regarding the characteristics that comprise an effective teacher, it will be difficult to advocate for specific tools and processes over others."[12]

ANALYZING THE JOB OF "TEACHER"

Despite, or even because of, the lack of agreement in the literature about what constitutes teaching effectiveness, it is advisable for school leaders responsible for hiring to systematically analyze the job of "teacher" to identify the essential tasks or duties of the job, as well as which knowledge, skills, abilities, or other characteristics (KSAOs) are needed to perform those tasks or duties. Through systematic analysis, these leaders can better identify what is needed for successful performance of job duties; this will inform the selection practices so that they are less likely to consider unrelated information (e.g., candidate attractiveness) and more likely to consider relevant information (e.g., knowledge of pedagogy) when hiring new teachers. This systematic analysis of a job is referred to as *job analysis,* and while there are several methods for conducting a formal job analysis, they all share an identical objective: identify the major activities and job requirements for a specific job and then identify the individual KSAOs needed to perform that job.

In 2010, our firm, 3D Group, worked with a school district to improve its teacher hiring process. At the outset, we conducted a detailed job analysis with teachers from more than thirty-five of the highest performing schools within this and one other district (based on comparisons to national norms for standardized test scores, recent test score improvements, and the input of the district administrators) in order to identify critical activities/tasks teachers perform on the job and the relevant KSAOs required to perform them. Our initial research included multiple sources, including existing job descriptions for teaching jobs, existing job analysis data on teachers, the U.S. Department of Labor's Occupational Information Network (ONET) database summary reports for teacher and teacher-related jobs, and previous research 3D Group had conducted with other schools. We then conducted focus groups with subject matter experts (SMEs) who were nominated as high performing teachers and principals from the thirty-five schools. Next, we shadowed teachers in the classroom and also conducted one-on-one interviews with the top performing teachers. From this research we identified five major duty areas— a high-level "collection of [related] tasks all directed at the general goals of a job"—for the job of teacher:[13]

- Design and implement effective strategies to develop learners

- Create and maintain a positive and safe learning environment
- Use evaluative and assessment data
- Demonstrate professionalism
- Perform administrative responsibilities

Next, we compiled a list of tasks that teachers perform related to these five, very broad duty areas using input from SMEs. This step of the research resulted in fifty-five tasks that effective teachers must perform. We conducted additional SME teacher interviews, classroom observations, and focus groups. Based on these additional sources of data, we compiled a more manageable list of the most important tasks. Finally, we asked a large sample of teachers to rate each of these tasks on the time they spent performing it ("Was this a frequently performed task?"), its difficulty, and the potential consequences of error ("If performed incorrectly, were the consequences large?") in order to determine each task's level of importance to the job. This last step allowed us to rank the tasks by level of importance. As a result of our research, we created a smaller, final list of forty-four tasks deemed critical to the teacher job.[14]

Next, 3D Group developed a list of potential KSAOs that would be needed to perform these tasks. We used focus groups of SMEs to reconfirm the final list of teacher tasks and to refine the list of KSAOs needed to perform the tasks. SMEs then rated each KSAO on whether it was necessary to have, needed before hire ("Must the teacher possess this attribute or skill before hire or can it be acquired on the job?"), the extent to which not having the KSAO would result in negative consequences, and whether the KSAO distinguished superior workers from average ones. Further research with teachers and data analysis revealed a final list of twenty-nine KSAOs deemed important for teacher selection.[15]

It is important to note that this list of twenty-nine KSAOs may be specific to the schools that participated in this study. While much of the information collected would extend to most school settings, we acknowledge that each school is different and has its own special culture and set of values.

WHAT MAKES AN EFFECTIVE TEACHER AT YOUR SCHOOL?

The job analysis results define a starting point for better understanding what teachers do and which qualities they need to perform their work. It seems reasonable, however, to assume that the behaviors that constitute effective teaching differ across situations and that teachers might have to call forth different sets of behaviors to affect student success. There is support for this contention. For example, a study of fourth and fifth grade mathematics instruction found that the components of quality teaching, based on student performance, varied according to students' needs.[16] In particular, teachers who provided instruction to classes comprised mostly of students in the poverty range had to provide students with different representations of mathematical concepts, while teachers in classrooms with fewer students in poverty could rely more on having students use textbooks and standard worksheets to gain knowledge and were able to delve into more complex lessons.

These results demonstrate the distinction between *teacher quality* and *teaching quality*. Teacher quality is "the bundle of personal traits, skills, and understandings an individual brings to teaching, including dispositions to behave in certain ways,

such as intelligence, verbal ability, content knowledge, pedagogical knowledge, an understanding of learning and development, and adaptive expertise for responding to students'
needs."[17] In contrast, teaching quality "has to do with strong
instruction that enables a wide range of students to learn."[18]
Teacher quality contributes to teaching quality, but situational
characteristics, such as the level of teaching (e.g., high school
versus elementary school) or student ability (e.g., high ability
versus struggling students), also influence teaching quality.

Of course, what is needed for success in one school or situation might be different from what is needed in other schools.
For example, some researchers have proposed that the qualities
assessed during interviews should address situations unique
to a school. These researchers described an approach to using employment interviews in urban school districts and suggested that interview questions be tailored to assess attitudes
and predispositions that are essential to effectiveness in high-
attrition environments like urban schools.[19] They conducted
a validity study that included items representing various domains (e.g., working with others, knowledge of content, knowledge of teaching, and knowledge of students) and correlated
the scores on these interview questions with supervisor ratings
of teachers. They added a domain in the interview for teachers in urban districts, aptitude/suitability for urban teaching,
which included items that measured the candidate's knowledge
of urban communities, knowledge of urban schools (i.e., ineq-
uitable procedural and distributive processes of urban schools),
determination of skills she possesses that are needed for success in an urban environment, belief that obstacles like poverty
and poor home support can be overcome, projection of how her
personal life would be impacted by teaching in an urban envi-

ronment, and ability to develop relationships across differences and student interests (i.e., interaction with students). Each of the domains related to teacher performance ratings in the n = 30 sample of urban teachers. By far, the strongest predictor was knowledge of teaching (correlation of .65), followed by aptitude/suitability for urban teaching (.49), knowledge of students (.44), knowledge of content (.35), and working with others (.34).

At this point, you might be wondering, "What are the characteristics I should be assessing to make sure that I hire good teachers? Are the teachers at my school required to do the same things as teachers at other schools? Do we have similar views of quality or effectiveness?" These are good questions. As with many jobs, there is not a one-size-fits-all approach to defining and assessing employee qualities that result in success in all organizations. As the literature indicates, many sources agree on certain teacher qualities that represent success in the profession and that it is possible to systematically define the teacher job in terms of its critical tasks and the KSAOs needed to perform those tasks. However, other research warns that situational or environmental influences affect teaching practices, and that should be taken into account when looking at an individual district or school.

This means that each school should spend some time conducting its own research to determine what makes an effective teacher for that specific school's culture and special characteristics. Even if many of the above examples seem like a good fit for your organization, systematically identifying the most important KSAOs within your school(s) is a critical first step in building better selection tools.

It is important to note that you don't have to start from scratch. To help you on this research journey, we provide in table 2.1 a list of forty-nine KSAOs that 3D Group's research found were important to perform the job of teaching effectively. We suggest that you use this list as a starting point and then fine-tune it to fit the unique needs of your organization. As part of this evaluation process, you can follow the 3D Group procedure used in our 2010 study; but, at a minimum, you should whittle down our list of KSAOs to a more manageable number to measure during your selection process (ideally twenty to thirty) and ask SMEs within your district to consider if there are any KSAOs pertinent to your organization that are not on this list.

Table 2.1

List of teacher knowledge, skills, abilities and other characteristics (KSAOs)

1	***Education and training:*** Knowledge of principles and methods for curriculum design, teaching, and instruction for individuals and groups
2	***Subject area:*** Knowledge of his/her specific subject area; state and district standards; knows how to use rubrics provided for each subject area
3	***State standards:*** Knowledge of the state-mandated curriculum and testing standards
4	***Current educational practices:*** Knowledge of the most up-to-date educational strategies and best practices
5	***Legal regulations:*** Knowledge of state and federal regulations, including special education laws, privacy issues, and rights of the child
6	***Policies:*** Knowledge of state, district, and school procedures, policies, and administrative regulations
7	***Information gathering:*** Able to use available resources to identify and obtain instructional information
8	***Data interpretation:*** Able to use various sources of data to identify students' developmental needs
9	***Learning strategies:*** Able to select instructional methods and procedures appropriate for the situation; selects best methods and procedures for different cultures

10	**Critical thinking:** Able to use logic and reasoning to identify the strengths and weaknesses of alternative solutions, conclusions, or approaches to problems
11	**Problem sensitivity:** Able to tell when something is wrong or is likely to go wrong
12	**Personal organization:** Able to manage time, prioritize, organize, and plan in order to accomplish work
13	**Coaching and developing:** Able to identify the developmental needs of others by measuring performance against goals and helping them meet those goals and providing constructive feedback
14	**Communication:** Able to share information with others in a clear and concise manner; demonstration of professionalism verbally and nonverbally; demonstration of respect and courtesy when communicating with others
15	**Listening:** Able to listen attentively to others and extract relevant information
16	**Interpersonal relationships:** Able to establish and maintain effective working relationships with others (e.g., teachers, administrative staff, parents, students)
17	**Lesson planning:** Able to plan future lessons and identify any needed resources
18	**Problem solving:** Able to analyze information and evaluate results in order to select the best solutions to problems
19	**Developing objectives and strategies:** Able to establish long-range learning objectives and specify the strategies and actions necessary to achieve them.
20	**Resourcefulness:** Able to locate and use available resources to the advantage of students
21	**Originality:** Able to generate innovative ideas about a given topic or situation or to develop creative ways to solve a problem
22	**Initiative:** Able to begin and complete a plan or task
23	**English language:** Knowledge of the English language, including the meaning and spelling of words, rules of composition, and grammar
24	**Strategy implementation:** Able to use the most appropriate instructional methods and materials to support student learning.
25	**Classroom technologies:** Able to use classroom technologies to support student activities and learning
26	**Balanced instruction:** Able to balance instructional activities effectively so that all material is adequately covered
27	**Management of others:** Able to plan and direct activities, including assigning work, adhering to schedules, and managing behavior

continued

Table 2.1 *continued*

28	**Adaptability:** Able to respond appropriately to unanticipated changes, to demonstrate flexibility
29	**Psychology:** Knowledge of human behavior and development; individual differences in ability, personality, and interests; learning and motivation; and behavioral and affective disorders
30	**Safety and security:** Knowledge of relevant equipment, policies, and procedures necessary to protect people and property and an understanding of classroom safety
31	**Health and wellness:** Knowledge of healthy child development, including physical development and understanding basic nutritional needs
32	**Students with disabilities:** Able to use assistive technologies to accommodate students with disabilities
33	**Environment:** Able to strategically organize classroom, including furniture, interactive materials, and learning aids
34	**Inclusiveness:** Able to treat others with respect regardless of individual differences
35	**Authority:** Able to respect and concern oneself with the rules and regulations in place, including authority figures
36	**Testing and assessment:** Knowledge of test and assessment design, including relating testing to state and district standards and correlating testing to instruction
37	**Data analysis:** Knowledge of basic data analysis required for administering and interpreting assessments
38	**Data use:** Able to use technology to access data, download reports, and manipulate data
39	**Deductive reasoning:** Able to apply general rules to specific problems to produce answers that make sense
40	**Inductive reasoning:** Able to combine pieces of information to form general rules or conclusions, including finding relationships among seemingly unrelated events
41	**Impartiality:** Able to act objectively and impartially
42	**Integrity:** Able to act honestly and ethically and maintain confidentiality
43	**School direction:** Knowledge of school's mission, vision, values, and goals

44	**Professional behavior:** Knowledge of what constitutes professional behavior and ability to demonstrate it
45	**Personal development:** Able to accept evaluative feedback in order to support professional growth and work to continuously improve him/herself
46	**Reflectiveness:** Able to take time to reflect on situations and actions
47	**Dependability:** Reliable and responsible, as evidenced by following through on commitments, meeting deadlines, arriving on-time, etc.
48	**Clerical matters:** Knowledge of administrative and clerical procedures and systems
49	**Administrative systems:** Able to use word processing programs, manage files and records, design forms, understand basic office procedures and terminology, and use school grading programs and other mandated programs and systems

Person-Job Fit Versus Person-Organization Fit

Candidates that meet the requirements of the job should be able to perform the tasks by demonstrating the appropriate job-specific KSAOs. This is known as *person-job (PJ) fit.* However, when picking your KSAOs, you may want to make sure that in addition to meeting job-related requirements, any teaching candidate also has the KSAOs required to fit into the organization. Consider past situations in which people have successfully been hired into a job and succeeded at the job but failed to fit into the organization. Suppose, for example, that a software engineer with impeccable skills takes a job at a start-up software company. He has recently graduated from an advanced program at a prestigious university and has all the KSAOs needed to perform the tasks. However, the start-up values teamwork; all the engineers work together on projects, and individual contributions are combined so that only team results are recognized. There is nothing wrong with this approach, but the new engineer is accustomed to, and prefers, working alone and would rather be held accountable for only his contribution. He has all the KSAOs needed for the work, but he likely will not succeed in this organizational environment. Notice, too, that this same circumstance could apply to a school that emphasizes team teaching and collaboration versus one which prefers that teachers stay focused on their own classrooms.

The fit with the unique attributes of the organization is known as *person-organization (PO) fit*. Schools may differ in terms of their personalities or organizational culture, how they expect teachers to interact with parents, whether they are located in rural or suburban or urban areas, or a myriad of other situational variables.

Meta-analytic research has established that both PJ and PO fits predict organizational outcomes.[20] Employees with higher PJ fit have higher job satisfaction (correlation of .56) and organizational commitment (.47) and are less likely to plan on quitting their job (–.46). PJ fit also correlates positively with co-worker satisfaction (.32), supervisor satisfaction (.33), and identification with the organization (.36).

Like the software engineer, it is important to consider a teacher's fit with the organization, even if she fits the job. PO fit correlates with job satisfaction (.44) and organizational commitment (.51).[21] Those with higher PO fit are less likely to quit (–.35). In addition, PO fit correlates with coworker satisfaction (.39), supervisor satisfaction (.33) and trust in management (.43). PJ fit is a better predictor of job satisfaction, while PO fit is a better predictor of organizational commitment. Interestingly, PJ fit correlates with job performance (.20), but PO fit shows very little relationship with job performance (.07). Those fitting the job may be more successful performers, but without PO fit they have fewer positive attitudes and are less likely to stay.

Of course, it would be much easier to have one way of defining teacher effectiveness that all schools can use to hire. This would allow us to use singular, standardized tools to hire teachers for every school. Reality shows us, though, that we need to tailor our approach to the unique needs of each school, or at least each school district. This doesn't mean that we can't make informed decisions about selecting teachers. Some authors have quipped when referring to the use of judgment in the selection process that "while this may have the advantage of giving principals the discretion to make decisions based on the particular needs of their school, there is clearly room for principals to make better decisions with improved processes and better prioritizing of tools."[22]

SUMMARY

To begin making improvements to your selection process, you must begin thinking about what makes an effective teacher. In addition, it is important to pay attention to those characteristics that will make teachers especially effective working within your school's culture. In this chapter we describe a process for identifying the essential tasks teachers perform and the KSAOs required to perform those tasks. It also includes a longer list of teacher KSAOs that districts can use as a starting place when considering what to measure as part of the selection process.

3

CHOOSING SELECTION TOOLS

Factors to Consider

Effective selection tools can provide school districts with information about candidates that can be useful in making hiring decisions. But some tools are better than others. Before using a selection tool, it is important to better understand how well the tool is measuring characteristics of the candidates and whether those characteristics are useful in identifying the best candidates.

RELIABILITY AND VALIDITY

Suppose that a school district uses no selection tools in hiring teachers. Candidates are not asked to complete application forms, submit to testing, or interview for jobs. Instead, the school district simply hires applicants who express interest in vacant positions randomly or on a first-come-first-served basis. This selection process—with no information about a candidate's job-relevant knowledge, skills, or abilities—will likely result in

43

overall low-quality teaching and limited student learning. The school district will miss many of the talented teachers in the applicant pool and fill at least some vacancies with candidates unable to perform the essential teaching functions. The percentage of proficient teachers hired using such a method reflects the recruiting pool performance base rate, the approximate percentage of proficient teachers who are likely to consider applying for a teaching position with that organization. Considering the recruiting pool base rate acknowledges that even with no screening tools, some of the teachers hired will be proficient. At a minimum, hiring tools can be defined as effective when they can demonstrate improved hiring decisions beyond the current recruiting pool base rate. And, of course, the best tools are the ones that exceed the base rate the most when it comes to their ability to differentiate good hires from bad hires. So, the better the hiring tools used, the fewer hiring mistakes will be made.

Of course, it is unrealistic to think that a school district would hire teachers with no attempt at screening. Most schools and school districts use a variety of tools for choosing teachers.[1] Applicant screening tools are a means for achieving an outcome—in this case, predicting teacher effectiveness. However, using tools does not *guarantee* us good information. The data from less effective tools does little to help us choose the best teachers; without useful data informing our decisions, we might do just as well randomly selecting candidates to fill jobs. So, how do we know that the test or interview we are using is "good?" Selection tools are most useful when the data obtained from them are consistent, or reliable, and when the inferences we make on the basis of that data are valid.

Measurements often include at least some variability due to random error. Let's assume, for example, that you measure a piece of paper with a ruler. The length of the paper remains constant. Your tool, the ruler, also remains constant as a measurement instrument; it does not change in size or in how well it measures objects. However, suppose that you hold the ruler different ways when measuring the paper, the paper slides, or you forgot your glasses and find it difficult to read the small markings on the ruler. These factors influence the measurements you record, and they represent error in measurement. A true score exists for the length of paper (e.g., 11 inches), but your observed measurements are 10.5 inches, 11.2 inches, and 11.1 inches. The measurement variability reflects error. Reliability is the degree to which ratings or measurements are free from random error.[2] In the context of teaching proficiency, each teacher has a true proficiency level. When we use selection tools, we are trying to measure the absolute ability of each teacher as accurately as possible.

When we misuse tools or use screening tests that are not perfectly accurate, our measurements contain errors. One of the first priorities when choosing a screening tool is to minimize error in the measurement procedures as well as error intrinsic to the tool. For example, unstructured interviews that ramble and don't include note taking tend to have more errors than structured interviews with notes. One error introduced during these interviews comes out of asking each candidate different questions, just like each time we measure the paper we hold the ruler a different way.

Inter-rater Reliability

Potential for error is even greater when using tools such as interviews and observations that rely on human judgment or inference. For example, a school hiring committee (principal, two

45

teachers, an HR representative) interviews two candidates for a teacher position. Committee members agree on their assessment of Candidate A. Each interviewer scores the responses of Candidate A as strong. However, they do not agree on how strong Candidate B's responses are. The principal and one of the teachers rate Candidate B's responses as strong; the other teacher and the HR representative rate B's responses as weak. Which candidate should be selected? What is the correct rating of B's responses?

The interviewers agreed on ratings for Candidate A; their ratings show consistency or high reliability across interviewers. Candidate B's ratings exhibit low reliability across interviewers. Potentially, all interviewers observed the candidate at the same time and heard the same response. What could cause these differences in ratings or this lack of reliability? The ratings, or observed scores, reflect the candidate's actual level of competence as well as error. Unlike the ruler example, the true score might include not only the competence on what is being evaluated but also systematic error. What is systematic error?[3] Suppose the hiring committee from our example would like to know if our candidates can form a lesson plan quickly while under stress. The committee can assume that each candidate has a true level of competence in forming a lesson plan under typical circumstances. But asking candidates to do this as part of the interview situation introduces stress or anxiety, and the stressful situation of the interview introduces systematic error that affects all candidates and is beyond the competence of developing a lesson plan. But if the committee is interested in assessing lesson planning under stress or time pressure, this systematic error becomes part of the true score.[4] Differences in candidates' scores on the interview would then represent the systematic variance, which includes differences due to true score and systematic error as well as random error.[5] If random error can be minimized, then the different scores would more purely reflect meaningful differences among candidates.

In the example, we can see that raters consistently or reliably scored the performance of Candidate A. However, the variability in Candidate B's scores suggests the presence of random error. These scores are unreliable. It could be that Candidate B reminds the principal of her brother and her high rating reflects her fondness for the candidate based on this similarity. The HR representative, however, receives a text message during the interview that distracts him and he hears only part of Candidate B's response to the lesson planning question. As a result of his distraction, he gives Candidate B a low score on the question. In this situation, the ratings (observed scores) do not reflect the candidate's true level of lesson planning capacity under stressful conditions, or systematic variability. Instead, the ratings include random error introduced by the raters. This random error clouds the hiring committee's potential for identifying meaningful differences between the candidates. If a measurement of knowledge, skills, or abilities reflects mostly random error instead of actual competence, there is no assurance that the best teachers are being chosen. Robert Guion summed up the importance of reliability to making hiring decisions: "If individual differences in scores are substantially attributable to random error, no other point of argument—even an attractive one—matters very much."[6] As such, one critical goal when developing hiring processes is to eliminate random error. The goal is to create tools and processes that measure all candidates equally so that comparisons among candidates reflect true differences in their abilities rather than unreliable measurement.

Other Types of Reliability

Reliability of scores also can be assessed over time (test-retest reliability), across different versions of a selection method (parallel forms reliability), and in responses to items within a selection method (internal consistency). For example, someone's personality is stable over time.[7] If a candidate is given a personality test today and then the same test in six months, it's expected that the two scores would be similar. Some differences could occur due to random error, such as the candidate having to take the test in a hot room during the second administration or the candidate having little sleep before taking the test the first time. However, because personality is relatively stable, the scores would be similar and show consistency across time. If the scores vary substantially, they are unreliable or inconsistent and should not be relied on as indicators of true personality type.

We have similar concerns when we use different forms of a selection method and they yield different scores for the same person. For example, if we measure a candidate's knowledge of conflict resolution techniques with two different interview questions and the candidate is scored differently on these two questions, we have low reliability across the questions. Therefore, we can't assume that we can use the questions interchangeably with candidates, because they might result in different scores for the same quality answers.

Internal Consistency Reliability

Internal consistency results mainly from how a selection tool is developed. If a tool has high internal consistency, then the respondents generally address the test items (or questions) in the same manner. For example, if you are interested in assessing how extraverted or introverted people are, you would ask questions to assess this personality characteristic, such as whether someone prefers to be with others or to be alone, is energized when engaging with others, or tends to start conversations with strangers. Your first respondent is consistent; she prefers to be with others, finds engaging with others energizing, and often starts conversations with strangers. Your second respondent also is consistent; he prefers to be alone, he finds engaging with others draining, and he rarely initiates conversations with strangers. Each item serves as a sample of how extroverted or introverted a person is. In this case, the respondents gave consistent responses: the first respondent consistently marked test items that suggest extroversion, and the second respondent marked items that were consistent with introversion. Internal consistency refers to how consistently each respondent answers the questions. If the test items are true samples of the attribute being measured, the respondent will act consistently across those items. Unreliability means that there are one or more test items that respondents answer differently from the other items. This could mean that the questions are not truly reflective of the attribute being measured.

If a selection method yields unreliable results, it cannot be used effectively. Unreliability means that the results are inconsistent or fluctuating. If scores or ratings on a stable characteristic fluctuate, error is probably being measured more than a true score. This means that information gathered about the candidates cannot be used. Without reliable measures, hiring decisions cannot be improved above the recruiting pool base rate.

Validity

While measurement reliability is essential, it turns out that reliability isn't enough to accurately predict job performance.

Even if a selection tool gives reliable scores, the characteristic being measured might have little bearing on how well the person teaches students. If we measure the wrong things, our decisions could result in the same outcome as hiring randomly; hiring decisions would be based on candidate scores, but the scores aren't relevant to the job. For example, suppose we make job offers based on physical attractiveness. We might agree on which candidates are attractive, but attractiveness does not relate to how well the candidates can teach students and foster learning. In this case, we measure attractiveness reliably—our ratings agree—but physical attractiveness is not a valid measure of teacher effectiveness. Ratings of physical attractiveness, however, might serve as a valid measure for selecting fashion models. Therefore, validity isn't a property of the selection tool (e.g., physical attractiveness measure); instead, it represents what we infer from the test scores.[8]

Validity addresses two issues: score interpretation and score use. The first is a descriptive inference, referring to how scores are interpreted for the selection method, and the second relates to action, how the score is used for making decisions.[9] Suppose that a principal asks candidates a number of questions about addressing conflicts, such as how they would handle conflicts with students, parents, and other teachers. The principal then rates each candidate's answers using a rating (e.g., 1 to 5) based on how well the responses address key points for resolving conflicts effectively. The ratings are summed to form an overall score. We can more accurately interpret the overall score if each of the questions accurately reflects conflict and if we score the questions based on how conflicts should be resolved. In addition, we would need to determine if the scores help us predict which candidates would be better teachers. If those who score higher on the conflict resolution tool perform better on the job than those who scored lower, then the inferences we make about job performance using the conflict resolution scores tend to be valid. However, if high and low scorers do equally well on the job, our inferences are not valid and, again, the tool is not helping us improve over decisions above the recruiting pool base rate.

Validity often is measured using correlations. The correlations represent the relationship between scores on a selection method (e.g., interview) and an important outcome or criterion (e.g., job performance, student success). Correlations range from –1.0 to 1.0, with correlations near 0 indicating little relationship between two variables. A correlation near 1.0 or –1.0 suggests a strong relationship between two variables. Typically, when comparing the relationship between performance and scores on selection tools, correlations of .15 and below can be considered weak predictors of performance; correlations between .15 and .30 can be considered moderate predictors; and correlations between .31 and .50 can be considered strong predictors. Correlations for individual instruments greater than .50 are rare and very strong.

Suppose we're testing candidates to hire history teachers. We could test the job candidates' knowledge of history and then measure their students' success in the course. We might find a very strong correlation, such as .48, indicating that the teachers who scored higher on the knowledge test had students who performed better in class, while teachers with lower scores on the knowledge test had students who did not perform as well in class. It is not a perfect correlation, but it indicates a strong positive relationship between the two sets of data. Figure 3.1 shows an example of such a test-to-performance correlation using a scatter plot of one hundred hypothetical teachers.

Figure 3.1
Test to performance: Strong correlation

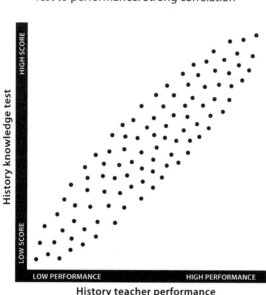

As figure 3.1 illustrates, the relationship between these two measures is not perfect; rather, it is a strong positive correlation. The pattern suggests a hiring tool that will be a valuable asset in predicting teacher performance; hiring decisions using this test will be valid.

Not all assessments are predictive of job performance, however. In fact, it is quite possible that there is a very weak or near zero correlation between current hiring tools and subsequent job performance (which is one reason to conduct research to ensure the validity of each hiring tool as described in chapter 9, section 3). In this case, we find that high scores on the test (or hiring tool) are unrelated to job performance. For example, knowing that an applicant had a high score on a history test might not predict job performance for science teachers. Figure 3.2 illustrates a near-zero correlation between the history test and job performance.

The near zero correlation illustrated in figure 3.2 would suggest that the history test provides no predictive information whatsoever when trying to hire science teachers. Hiring decisions made using this test will not be valid. An example of a negative correlation might be the relationship between scores on a conscientiousness test and absenteeism. Teachers who are more conscientious (based on their score on the test) are less likely to call in sick once they are hired, while teachers who score lower on conscientiousness items are more likely to call in sick. This is a negative relationship. The stronger the relationship between

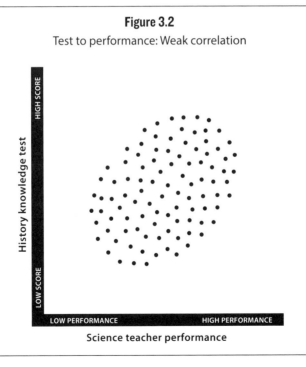

Figure 3.2
Test to performance: Weak correlation

variables, the more likely we can use one variable to predict the other. Typically, the validity of a test for predicting an important outcome, such as job performance, does not exceed .50, and most validity coefficients top out at around .30.[10]

Effects of Validity on Hiring Mistakes. The reason for using any screening tool to make hiring decisions is to decrease hiring mistakes. The simple fact is that the better a given tool predicts job performance (that is, the stronger it correlates with job performance), the fewer hiring mistakes will be made when the tool is used to screen candidates. Naturally, most principals and hiring managers focus their concern on avoiding bad hires. After all, a teacher who does not succeed on the job requires considerable effort on the part of principals, HR staff, and even colleagues who may have to take up the slack. Hiring mistakes that are often overlooked are those where qualified candidates are not chosen. These mistakes reflect missed opportunities. In this situation, the district has expended effort in attracting and recruiting the applicant, but by using an imperfect screening tool they have not accurately detected the candidate's true proficiency. Figure 3.3 illustrates the types of errors districts can make when using a screening tool to make hiring decisions. Most, but not all, of the 50 applicants in figure 3.3 who were selected (those above the passing score) will be effective teachers.

Using this test to hire teachers would result in 43 good hires and only 7 bad hires. Of those candidates who were rejected, only 9 should have been hired. All in all, this test would be an excellent tool for hiring teachers. While we don't have an exact figure, the correlation presented here is quite strong, probably somewhere in the .50 range.

Figure 3.3

Screening tool with strong correlation to job performance

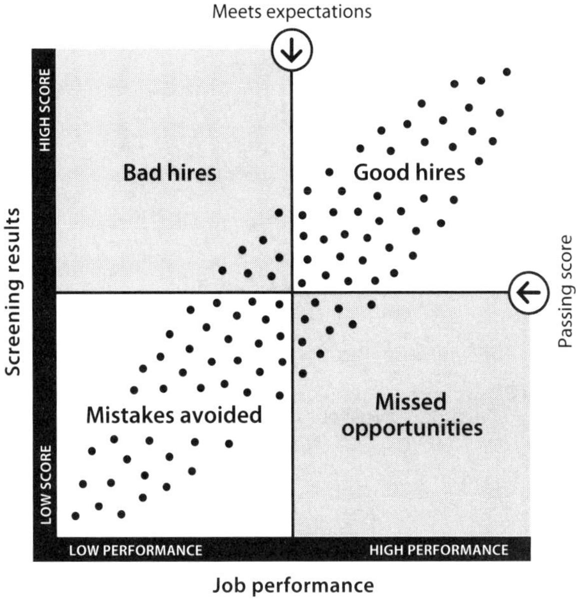

So what happens when a district uses a test that does *not* correlate well with teacher performance? When screening tools do not correlate with teacher performance, they don't add any predictive information and they result in considerably more hiring mistakes (of both types) than when a highly correlated test is used. Figure 3.4 illustrates the expected effects of using a test with a weak correlation (below .15) to screen candidates. In this example, the test did manage to screen out 31 bad hires and identify 31 good hires, so it wasn't completely worthless. The problem lies in the fact that more than a third (17) of the teachers recommended for hire by this test (all 48 applicants who scored above the passing score line) turned out to be bad

Figure 3.4

Screening tool with weak correlation to job performance

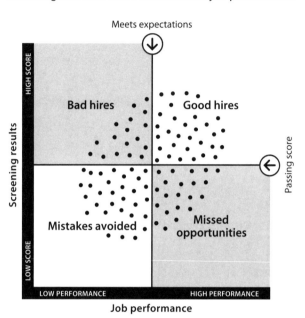

hires. Clearly, using this test to hire teachers would not be rec-ommended; we can only imagine the impact on student learn-ing and school success if more than a third of new hires failed on the job. Figure 3.4 also illustrates an often overlooked hiring mistake: missed opportunities. In this example, 21 candidates were rejected who would have turned out to be great teachers. As a consequence, using the same screening tool that accepts over a third bad hires, the district would be rejecting more than 40 percent of the qualified teachers who applied. It is hard to say which mistake—making bad hires or missed opportunities—has a larger negative effect on the quality of education.

VALIDITY OF VARIOUS SELECTION METHODS

A wide range of selection tools can be used for gathering information about applicants. These tools can be well established and have a proven track record for success, or they can be highly subjective with very weak validity, with many having no evidence to support their use. Some organizations have even gone to extremes by using highly suspect tools like handwriting analysis or lie detector tests to predict employee behavior without researching the validity of subsequent hiring decisions. Of course, not all screening tools need to narrowly predict performance. Some, such as basic application forms, references, and background checks, help schools avoid hiring a teacher with glaring deficiencies (e.g., lacking credentials, criminal history), but they do not differentiate the best candidates from those who would perform poorly on the job. The best of these tools have been researched extensively to understand how well they typically improve hiring decisions. Table 3.1 displays validity coefficients between various types of hiring tools and job performance to demonstrate the range of validity levels that research has demonstrated.

While we explore research and methods for building and applying several of these in detail in subsequent chapters, we focus here on the best and most practical selection tools that predict teacher performance: structured interviews, job simulation tasks, and teaching observation.

Interviews

School officials often regard the face-to-face interview as the most important aspect of the teacher hiring process.[11] Research supports the notion that interviews can provide information that helps choose high performing candidates. However, not

Table 3.1
Typical tool-to-performance validity levels for a wide range of hiring tools

Hiring tools	Correlation to performance	Meta-analysis source
Structured interview	.57	Huffcutt & Arthur (1994)
Work sample	.54	Hunter & Hunter (1984)
Cognitive ability	.51	Schmidt & Hunter (1998)
Job knowledge	.48	Hunter & Hunter (1984)
Situational interviews	.43	Huffcutt et al. (2003)
Integrity tests	.34	Ones et al. (1993)
Grades	.32	Roth et al. (1996)
Job experience	.27	Quinones et al. (1995)
Reference checks	.26	Hunter & Hunter (1984)
Personality (conscientiousness)	.24	Hurtz & Donovan (2000)
Unstructured interview	.20	Huffcutt & Arthur (1994)
Personality (emotional stability)	.15	Hurtz & Donovan (2000)
Personality (agreeableness)	.12	Hurtz & Donovan (2000)
Education	.10	Hunter & Hunter (1984)
Personality (extraversion)	.09	Hurtz & Donovan (2000)
Personality (openness)	.06	Hurtz & Donovan (2000)
Graphology	.02	Schmidt & Hunter (1998)

Note: Authors of the meta-analyses statistically corrected these correlations to account for study artifacts such as range restriction; such statistical correlations invariably increase stated correlations to more accurately reflect true test criterion relationships.

all interviews work equally well in choosing successful job candidates. In a meta-analysis of studies representing eighty-six thousand employees across many industries, researchers found that situational interviews (e.g., asking candidates how they responded to a work-related situation in the past) have higher average validity (.50) for predicting job performance than do nonsituational job-related interviews (.39) or psychological interviews (.29), in which personal traits like enthusiasm are assessed.[12] Similarly, research found a validity coefficient of .51 between situational-based structured interview questions and job performance for mill employees.[13] They also found a validity coefficient of .39 between experience-based structured interview questions and job performance for this same population. Furthermore, structured interviews, in which questions are standardized across candidates, are more valid (.44) than unstructured interviews (.33).[14] However, the authors of the study suggested that these results could be inflated, because the only unstructured interviews they considered were those with scales that raters use to assess responses. Many unstructured interviews have no rating scales.

Other research estimated a much larger difference in validity between structured (.61) and unstructured interviews (.05) in predicting sales dollars as the performance criterion.[15] But can we really expect results with insurance sales people to apply to teachers? Yes and no. Obviously, the same questions can't be used for sales people as teachers. Clearly this would not work. Rather, we are suggesting the same process should be used—specifically, structured behavioral interviewing. The actual questions used for teachers need to be tailored to the specific knowledge, skills, and abilities that are required to succeed as a teacher. Indeed, research with school districts has provided evidence that structured interviews can predict teacher performance.[16] Some research shows school principals report choosing structured over unstructured interviews.[17]

Unstructured interviews conducted by a panel have higher validity (.21) than unstructured interviews administered individually (.11), and structured interviews have similar validity when conducted by a panel (.33) versus individually (.35).[18] However, considering all types of interviews, those conducted by a panel or board are less valid (.32) than those conducted individually with a candidate (.43).[19] These panel interviews generally cost more to conduct, so they need higher validity to be cost effective.[20] Yet, most school principals surveyed in one research study reported using panel interviews instead of individual interviews, and most were structured.[21]

Job Simulations

How job candidates perform on simulations often predicts performance outcomes. Depending on the job, simulations may include such activities as in-basket exercises (a test that simulates tasks employees would likely perform at their desk, such as prioritizing and ordering responses to a large number of e-mails), role playing, or essay writing. Job simulations may be verbal or physical; both predict training performance and proficiency criteria with typical validity coefficients ranging from .45 to .62.[22] Job simulations can be particularly popular (and predictive) in public safety jobs, where physical strength and endurance can be measured. One simulation for teachers' work is the portfolio, which represents a sample of work. Although portfolios are often required in teacher education, many employers do not specifically ask for them to be included for teacher selection.[23] Career services professionals, who act as a liaison between education graduates and employing school districts, generally see the portfolios as a marketing tool rather than an evaluative tool in the school's selection process and report that they are used rarely for making decisions about candidates.[24] Other similar simulations, such as sample lesson plans and use of videotaped performance, are also only rarely used.[25] These tools generally are considered costly because they require decision makers to review them or to create and rate hypothetical scenarios.[26] However, the use of such samples does accurately predict performance for many jobs.[27]

Job Performance Assessments

What better way to know how a teacher will interact with students than to observe the teacher? Performance assessments require that a candidate complete a set of tasks that sample the performance domain.[28] Unlike viewing a recorded videotape or examining a portfolio, teacher observation requires that the candidate perform teaching duties live while being observed and rated by the principal or the hiring committee. The use of such performance assessments allows the potential employer to sample the candidate's behavior in a setting that resembles the actual work environment.[29] Job candidates generally view performance assessments more favorably than more traditional tests.[30] In addition, observations are usually reserved for candidates already trained in the job. The typical relationship between work sample performance (e.g., observation) and job performance has been estimated at .41.[31] Despite potential for high validity and positive applicant reactions, most principals surveyed in one study indicated that they do not conduct teacher observation because of time constraints.[32]

PRACTICAL CONSIDERATIONS

Teaching positions often attract a large pool of candidates.[33] In one study, principals reported that they generally reduce the number of potential candidates by using professional attributes that are easily verified, such as teaching experience and grade point average. Then, during a face-to-face interview, principals focus on personal characteristics such as communication ability and confidence.[34] The struggle for many schools is how to reduce the large pool of candidates to a small group of highly qualified hires to fill positions. Valid selection methods help us minimize hiring mistakes, but even if valid tools are used, managing the sheer volume of applicants during a hiring period introduces a number of important practical considerations related to the design of a district's hiring process.

Selection Ratios and Base Rates

Valid selection methods yield more accurate predictions. However, schools face additional realities in the selection process to consider that impact selection outcomes. Two of these are selection ratio and incumbent base rate. The selection ratio is the percentage of applicants hired. For example, a selection ratio of 90 percent means that the school district is hiring ninety of every 100 applicants. In this case, it is possible that the need for teachers outweighs the desire to hire the very best. If the selection ratio is high and the district is hiring almost everyone who applies, the validity of the selection methods will have less effect than if the selection ratio is low, and the district can be more selective. They might identify the very best candidates, but the need for teachers means that they hire not only the very best but also candidates with much lower qualifications. However, if the selection ratio is 9 percent instead of 90 percent, they're generally hiring about 9 of every 100 applicants. They can be selective in the candidates they hire. This is when higher validity is usually more advantageous. Selection methods with higher validity help to more accurately identify the better candidates without having to consider candidates who are less qualified. Usually, more benefit is derived from using valid selection methods if the selection ratio is kept low. One way to decrease the selection ratio and to be more selective is to limit the number of candidates hired, though this might not be feasible given the needs of the school district. The second method is to increase the number of applicants. However, if a district attracts only high-quality candidates as applicants, then decreasing the selection ratio isn't necessary; even if the district hired all the applicants, they would all be successful.

Incumbent base rate (which differs from the recruitment pool base rate) refers to the percent of employees in the job who are performing successfully. For districts trying to improve their teachers' overall performance levels, consideration of the current incumbent base rate across the district may affect decisions about how beneficial a new hiring system might be. Many factors, including selection, training, and performance management programs, can contribute to a district's incumbent base rate. For example, a school might select high-quality candidates using its selection system, provide all teachers additional training in the knowledge and skills important for teaching, make available multiple development opportunities, and then provide ongoing valuable feedback about their performance. That school may have a 100 percent incumbent base rate, suggesting that everyone who is hired is successful. In this case, adding a more valid selection method to the selection system will not improve schoolwide outcomes. However, if the base rate is lower, there is more opportunity for improvement, and a more valid selection method could result in the hiring of more employees who will be successful.

Even in low base rate schools, it may be worth examining what factors are contributing to the performance problems.

For example, a district might have a sophisticated hiring system that results in new hires who are highly qualified and motivated, but once they are hired, the reward systems and supports for good teaching are simply not available. In this case, improving the hiring system will not improve outcomes, and resources would be better spent on improving the reward system and supports for good teaching. In a low- or medium-level base rate environment, districts are well served to conduct rigorous validation research on their selection instruments (and their training, rewards, and leadership). When a district examines the validity of these processes, it becomes easier to determine where improvements are needed. Research on hiring methods is an ideal place to start this inquiry, because it is often easier to draw strong conclusions about the validity of hiring tools than it is about how effective a particular training program or reward system might be.

The Hiring Funnel

Given the typical turnover in any given district, every spring there is a large push for hiring new teachers. In large districts, this can be an extremely daunting task. Sorting through large pools of applicants consumes valuable resources, including time and money. With careful planning about the sequence of hiring tools used to screen candidates, scarce resources can go much further. By putting your least expensive, most valid screening tools to use first, you can significantly decrease the total expense of the hiring process.

Imagine that the first step in the hiring process is an hour-long interview with a school principal (perhaps a school's most scarce commodity), and anyone who passed the principal interview would be asked to complete a short phone screen with an HR staff member (also not an abundant resource, typically, but likely more so than principals). If both interviews have the exact same pass rates, the district would be far better off putting the phone screen first. Looking at the overall flow of candidates in this way is known as the *hiring funnel* (see figure 3.5).

When managing the large volume of applicants at the peak hiring period, it is very important that districts consider the number of applicants passing through each phase of the funnel and understand how the pool narrows at each phase as a new selection tool is applied. School districts most often use a multiple hurdle approach to hiring, whereby applicants must clear each of many steps to be hired. The alternative would be

Figure 3.5

Multiple hurdle funnel for narrowing candidate pools

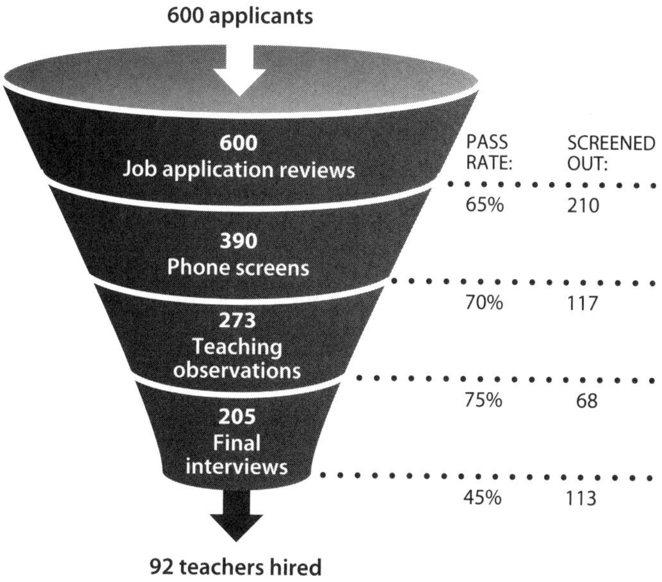

600 applicants

600 Job application reviews	PASS RATE:	SCREENED OUT:
	65%	210
390 Phone screens		
	70%	117
273 Teaching observations		
	75%	68
205 Final interviews		
	45%	113

92 teachers hired

to have all applicants complete all screening processes before making your hiring decision. This is considerably more expensive than the multiple hurdle method and therefore is not nearly as common. As illustrated in figure 3.5, the multiple hurdle method results in a narrowing of the candidate pool so that fewer and fewer candidates are considered viable. From a resource management standpoint, districts should use their least expensive screening tools first and the most expensive ones last.

In addition to designing the overall process to maximize resources, it may be possible to establish a target pass rate for each phase. For example, principals may state that they want only to interview two finalists for each position. The fictitious example used in figure 3.5 reflects just such a scenario: of the 205 candidates principals interviewed, they selected 92 teachers, or approximately half of the pool that cleared the first three hurdles. By using prior research about how candidates typically perform on each screening tool, districts can adjust the passing score for each tool to increase or decrease the expected volume of candidates that should pass through each phase. For example, you might establish the preferred volume of candidates at each phase and then set pass scores to accomplish this rate. Note that this requires maintaining records from previous screenings so expected pass rates can be established for each screening tool. Of course, even with good record-keeping, some variability in pass rates should be expected given that recruiting pool proficiency will vary somewhat from year to year.

One critical consideration in the hiring funnel is how valid the screening devices are and how many candidates they screen out. For example, at one school district we worked with, the initial pool of potential teachers in the spring of 2010 included more than 600 applicants. We put a quick but valid screening tool as the first step in the funnel and were able to reduce the initial pool to approximately 250 candidates. Our research confirmed that the tool had a moderately positive statistically significant correlation with teacher performance, and so we were confident that narrowing the candidate pool at this early phase would leave plenty of qualified candidates to get the district to its desired number of new hires. If a tool had been used in this fashion that had a poor correlation to teacher performance, the school would likely have not had enough remaining qualified teachers and would surely have made many bad hires.

WHO IS INVOLVED?

One of the key issues in hiring is the extent to which the process is centralized or decentralized.[35] Of twenty-eight superintendents surveyed in Canada, almost three-quarters (71 percent) indicated that the district organizes the hiring process, while 29 percent said that the district and the school share responsibilities for organizing.[36] Almost half (47 percent) indicated that the district and the school share responsibility for screening, while most of the interviewing is conducted at the school level.[37] Eighty-five percent indicated that the hiring decision was made by the school and the district working together, while 11 percent reported that the decision was made entirely at the school level.[38] Similarly, other research found that teams conducted teacher interviews 91.7 percent of the time; however, all principals they interviewed made the final hiring decision.[39]

Choosing the hiring team is a decision that must be made on a case-by-case—or school-by-school—basis depending on the available resources. Most of the school systems we work with are faced with a similar scenario: small selection ratio and

limited resources. For example, one school district was looking to hire approximately 110 teachers and facing nearly 900
job applicants (overall selection ratio of 12 percent). Their
principals were swamped with their own nonhiring duties but
wanted to be involved in interviewing a final round of candidates and in making a final decision. This particular organization centralized the first three hurdles of the selection process
to narrow the applicant pool, which allowed them to send only
highly qualified candidates to their busy principals for the final
two hurdles of the selection process. Each applicant first submitted to a central selection committee an application form
that contained a few screening questions. Those who cleared
this hurdle were selected for a structured phone interview with
a selection committee member. Conducting this interview over
the phone saved the school time and money. The candidates
who passed this phase were then invited to a central location to
participate in several job simulations, which included writing
a response to a common out-of-classroom scenario, generating
a writing sample, and taking a multiple-choice test to assess
planning and prioritizing. These simulations were designed to
be administered to a large group of applicants at one time—
again saving the school time and money. Finally, the school
district's centralized selection committee had a much smaller
number of applicants to now advance through the selection
the process and to send to each principal for the final hiring
decision. With each candidate, principals observed them teach
a short lesson and then conducted a face-to-face structured interview. The principal of each school then made a final hiring
decision after spending less than an hour and a half with each
candidate. While this may seem like a very small amount of
time to spend with a candidate, consider that each step a can-

didate passed was validated with research. As such, the overall validity of hiring decisions was .53. So, while principals' input was minimal compared to many typical hiring processes, the overall decisions turned out to be more accurate than most, and the investment of time by principals was less than might otherwise have been the case.

SUMMARY

Reliability and validity are essential components of any hiring tool. While reliability is necessary to ensure consistency of measurement, assessing the validity of decisions made using a hiring tool ensures that hiring mistakes are kept to a minimum. Even using highly valid, well-researched screening tools, our predictions will not be perfect; no hiring tool can provide perfectly valid inferences. While perfection may not be possible, we can minimize hiring mistakes by researching, documenting, and then using only the tools that *best* predict performance. Practical considerations related to the flow of candidates and who is involved in the hiring process can have a huge effect on the costs of a hiring system. Significant resources can be conserved if the appropriate research is conducted to ensure the optimal sequence of each screening tool as well as the ideal pass rate to achieve the desired number of teachers who are ultimately hired. Perhaps most significant is the question of incumbent base rate: districts with low incumbent base rates have far more to gain by improving their selection systems than districts with very high base rates.

4

GETTING THE MOST FROM APPLICATION FORMS

In many industries, paper-based applications have become a relic of the past, as individuals now include most of the information job applications were originally designed to capture in their curriculum vitae (CVs)/resumes. For many vacancies, applicants may never even see a job application form. But application forms can be a handy tool for selection when designed appropriately and when enough thought is put into the selection process as a whole.

Job applications are likely to be the most helpful for hiring scenarios with a high volume of applicants and low selection ratios. A selection ratio is computed by dividing the number of open positions by the total number of job applicants for these positions. If you have a large number of applicants applying for a limited number of positions (the ideal hiring scenario), application forms can be helpful because you can design them as valid screening tools. We've worked with organizations that faced hiring seventy-five teachers out of an applicant pool of 600 candidates (12 percent selection ratio). Districts trying to narrow a large pool of applicants into a small number of new hires can benefit greatly by using a quick and valid tool to reduce this pool of candidates to something more manageable. A well-designed application form is ideally suited for just this scenario. We've seen it implemented successfully and produce great results.

But why have application forms been disappearing for many jobs? For many individuals, the line between a resume and a CV has become quite blurred. Originally, resumes were intended to be more brief (one-to-two-page) summaries of an individual's work experience, job skills, and education background, and CVs were a much more detailed synopsis that included research and teaching experience, presentations and publications, awards, honors, affiliations, and other details. But as job markets become increasingly competitive, individuals have gone to extreme lengths to gain the attention of potential employers. Since often viewed as their one shot to leave a memorable first impression, applicants often wish to tell potential employers as much as possible about themselves and why they would be the perfect choice for the open position. This desire has led the information normally contained in resumes and the type of more detailed information typically contained in CVs to fuse and form into what's basically a personal marketing campaign. In effect, applicants are saying, "Let me take this opportunity to sell myself to you as quickly as possible, since it might be my only one!"

One member of the popular professional networking site LinkedIn actually included a CV that had been mocked up to look like a Google search engine results page. In the "Search" bar were adjectives like "creative," "unique," "hard working," and "talented," and then next to the ever-famous "Did you mean: _____" the individual's name appeared. We've seen examples of individuals renting out full billboards to advertise their job skills, and not too long ago we heard of someone who had his CV delivered to the head recruiter on the back of a Frisbee (turns out the head recruiter was a big fan of Frisbee golf). Basic linen stock paper resumes have now been replaced with interactive videos that feature the candidates speaking about themselves and contain embedded links to their CVs/ resumes. Applicants are able to demonstrate particular talents, job-related or not, and give the recruiter a sense for who they are on a more personal level. This seems to work very well for the more extroverted applicants, or those who enjoy taking center stage. One very ambitious job candidate we know sent a box full of T-shirts screen printed with his resume and photograph! As a member of the selection committee, what do you do when you get a T-shirt resume or a Frisbee application? How can you validly use this information to screen the applicant?

ADVANTAGES TO COLLECTING JOB APPLICATION DATA

So why collect job application forms? First, many candidates apply to schools at the district level. When the initial screening phase is centralized in this way, it is critical that standard information is collected on each candidate so that fair comparisons can be made and for data collection purposes (see "Adverse Impact Data").

Think about it. You are trying to determine which two of three candidates to grant a phone interview, Candidate A, B,

Adverse Impact Data

Adverse impact occurs when a different rate of selection in hiring, promotion, or other employment decisions works to the disadvantage of members of a race, sex, or ethnic group. It's important to collect demographic data on all job applicants to ensure that the selection tools are not discriminating against one of these classes. For example, one requirement for a particular job might be height. While seemingly neutral, this criteria will screen out more females than males over time. It's important to note that adverse impact is sometimes a reality for a particular job. If your selection tool does demonstrate adverse impact, then you must be able to legally prove that (1) the challenged practice is consistent with business needs and is job-related and (2) that an equally valid or job-related practice with less or no adverse impact could not have been used.*

*Arthur Gutman, *EEO Law and Personnel Practices* (Thousand Oaks, CA: Sage, 2000), 43–49.

or C? To make this decision, you need the same information on each candidate, otherwise you're almost certain to introduce random error into the decision-making process. Even in cases where candidates apply directly to the school it is essential to ensure that standard records on each applicant are collected. Ideally, these records would be captured from the individual schools at the district level and used in a more centralized manner to make the process more efficient in the long term. Standard job application forms are easy to scan, store, and use for data analysis purposes. One scanner and a software program can be used for standard forms, and those forms can then be entered into one database if needed.

Can you imagine trying to standardize 100 YouTube videos that candidates have submitted as their personal marketing campaigns? Even if your staff does have the time to view this many separate videos, how do you select the best one? Does a great video reflect great teaching or great showmanship, great classroom management or great salesmanship? Keep it simple and collect these same data from every candidate. To make it even simpler, collect this data online to streamline the process. This not only makes data entry obsolete, but it can provide live access to applicant information to the local school levels and can also make it easier to provide job applicants with more regular updates on their status. Some advantages to online application forms are:

- Job applicants can apply easily from any geographic location
- Once submitted, applicants can receive immediate acknowledgment that their application has been received
- The online system can be used to schedule interviews and provide applicants with live status of their application
- Allows HR to track volumes and manage resources
- Allows HR to track and code data easily

But make sure you consider the following when using an online application system:

- Are alternate forms for multiple languages required?
- Ensure proper design of any forms. For example, text boxes that are too small for adequate responses or toggle boxes that work incorrectly can be a major turn off to applicants and may appear "unfair."

- Instructions must be provided for every new section and they must be clear. If there is the smallest chance a particular section or question could be misunderstood, in reality someone will surely misunderstand it. We all know that even when providing clear instructions, there will always be some individuals who will not read them and will become confused.
- Online systems don't allow individuals to provide more individualized responses to questions. For example, if an applicant would like to explain why they have poor exam results, have a different certification than what is required, etc. . . . they can submit a letter with their paper/pencil application. With an online application, you often lose this flexibility, so provide a section for additional comments from the applicant.

Another important reason to collect job application data is that you can ask for information that the applicants might not provide in their resumes. Resumes are intentionally designed to highlight an applicant's strengths and hide any weaknesses. It's important to use both sources of information together. In the resume, an applicant is not likely to admit to a felony conviction or to having been fired from two jobs, but there are ways to uncover this information from the application form.

USING THE JOB APPLICATION FORM AS YOUR FIRST SCREENING TOOL

In most cases, a basic job application form provides very little job-specific information other than education and limited background experiences. In the above examples it might be possible to conclude that these individuals are outgoing or extra motivated, that they demonstrated some level of creativity or out-of-the-box thinking. But if you really want to get the most from your job application form, you need to think about ways you can begin to assess for job-related skills or abilities required for the job. Use your job application form as your first screening tool. To get the most value out of this effort, take the time to make the application a valid screening tool. This will involve collecting information from applicants that is predictive of teaching effectiveness and then developing a reliable and efficient way of evaluating that information to screen out the least qualified applicants.

Though rarely adding enough significant prediction to warrant using exclusively, application forms can be an essential component of a valid hiring system when combined with other tools. In general, the application tends to be viewed as a low-cost process that yields relatively superficial information and serves to reduce the candidate pool to a more manageable number.[1] A thoughtful use of screening application forms can identify clearly bad candidates, but with a little creativity they can add a small amount of valid prediction to the overall hiring system.

WHAT JOB APPLICATION FORMS CAN MEASURE

In a study of what components of application materials principals valued most, researchers found the cooperating teacher's letter of reference the most important, followed by the principal's and then the university supervisor's letters of reference.[2] These researchers found that transcripts were valued inconsistently. Principals reported that they felt they gained valuable information about the candidate through grades earned in their major area of study, previous experience teaching in the area of vacancy, and the letter of interest for the position (cover letter). The information most application forms are designed to collect from applicants includes the basic information you'll want to ensure you obtain from your candidates:

- Education: bachelor's degree, advanced degree
- Special certifications
- Relevant content knowledge
- Previous teaching experience
- Related teaching experiences (or nonacademic, job-related activities)
- Related leadership experiences
- Legally authorized to work in the United States
- Professional references

This is a cheap way to eliminate clearly unqualified candidates without spending more money to screen them further. Mostly, applications are used for identifying clear rejects, not making fine distinctions between the good and the great. You can use your application form to begin assessing job-related skills and to weed out the bad candidates early.

What can you expect to measure with your application form? First, there are candidate characteristics you can assess just by carefully reviewing the submitted application information. For example, some principals have reported using applications to assess more professional (versus personal) attributes of candidates. Noting whether the application form was typed or hand-written might indicate how "professional" the candidate intends to present himself.[3] Additional candidate characteristics that can be measured with application forms include:

- *Following directions/Attention to detail:* Did the candidate complete the application correctly and completely? If the applicant skipped a section completely or did not follow instructions correctly, this could indicate that they might be deficient in this area.
- *Writing skills:* Did the applicant make grammatical errors, typos, misspellings? Some of the longer, more open-ended questions on the application can provide you with an initial sense of writing skills and possibly even writing style.
- *Effort:* If your application form required some thoughtful responses or for the applicant to collect and present back data, did the applicant spend adequate time doing so? Is it obvious that the applicant put some extra effort into completing the application thoroughly?
- *Consistency:* Was the applicant consistent in his responses and the information he provided?

Remember that job application forms can be used to collect job-specific information. Here are some examples of the types of data you can collect to take that extra step when faced with a low selection ratio scenario, when you have a lot of candidates and few open positions:

- Personal examples of student data and obtaining classroom results
- Applied student data problem solving
- Domain knowledge specific to the position being applied for
- A short (under 5 minutes) video of the applicant teaching a lesson to a live classroom (This is very resource intensive, and you must spend a lot of time up front

ensuring your process is as efficient as possible, that videos be directly uploaded online, etc.)

In chapter 2 we mentioned person-organization (PO) fit and its importance to selecting the right candidate. PO fit is how well an individual fits with the unique attributes of an organization and it predicts job satisfaction and organizational commitment among other positive attitudes. You can use your job application to begin to assess for PO fit based on your school's culture. A few examples of what you can assess are:

- *Multicultural attitudes or experience:* "Have you had previous, documented success teaching ESL students?" or "What is the best way to manage behavior in mixed-race or multilingual classrooms?"
- *Attitudes toward test scores versus whole-child assessments:* "Do you use standardized test results in your classroom? If so, how?"
- *Attitude toward arts programs (for an arts magnet school):* "In less than 100 words, please describe why the arts are important to primary school education."

Say your school is located in a heavily urban area where over 90 percent of the students qualify for free lunches, and, like in many inner-city schools, these students must pass through a metal detector each morning as they enter the school grounds. You have a large number of applicants, and at this point in the hiring process you just want to select out the very poorest. A good question might be to simply ask the applicants if they are comfortable working in a school environment where students and faculty must pass through metal detectors each morning.

You don't want to waste your time on applicants who would respond "no" to this question.

Though this honest response may seem unlikely, remember that hiring is a game of large numbers. Some percentage of applicants will respond "no" to questions like these. Even if a simple yes/no question can screen out a very small number of applicants, the time savings can be valuable. If only .025 percent of applicants say "no" to this kind of knock-out question, with a pool of 1,000 this lets you knock out twenty-five people and gives you that much more time to spend on the applicants who deserve your attention. One trick to increasing the likelihood that people answer these seemingly obvious questions is to ask questions that are verifiable. For instance, applicants with criminal records or who have stolen from previous employers realize that you are likely to find out anyway, and some of them will save you the trouble of the background check by telling you up front.

We've also seen success with presenting a problem in the application form and asking the applicants to solve it. You might give the applicants classroom data and then present them with a problem scenario and ask them to write a brief description of how they would respond. A benefit of this approach is that early on you are capturing job-relevant data on your applicants. You must, however, keep your application forms highly secure or develop multiple sets of equivalent questions to ask the job applicants.

EXAMPLES OF SCREENING WITH JOB APPLICATION FORMS

A simple approach to early screening through the use of application forms is to ask straightforward questions that would quickly eliminate applicants (similar to the PO fit metal detector question mentioned above). For example, if your school believes that 100 percent of each class's students should make straight A's, and this is a critical value for all teachers to hold, then you could ask the following:

How many students do you believe have the potential to make straight A's in your classroom?

A. Probably 90%, depending on the class
B. 99%—no one is perfect
C. 100%—all students have that potential
D. 70%—some just don't have that potential

Anyone who selected A, B, or D as their answer would not progress to the next round of the selection process. While this hurdle is not likely to screen out many applicants, it is likely to catch a few mismatches and save your selection team some time in this process. We are not suggesting that you use this specific question but are simply providing an example for illustrative purposes (indeed, you could alter the question to indicate attitudes that grades are not as important as effort if that reflects the attitude you are trying to cultivate among your faculty).

A more rigorous approach would be to ask much more job-specific questions, perhaps tapping into more detailed domain knowledge for the position in question. In 2009, the Houston Independent School District (HISD) had more than 5,000 applicants. This is definitely a situation when it's desirable to quickly reduce the applicant pool to a more manageable number. In this case, HISD tagged only 12 percent (or 600) of the applicants as even qualified.[4] The district made sure it wasn't expending too many resources on the unqualified candidates by screening them out early. Elementary and middle school applicants without certification in a specific subject were required to pass a fifth grade math test to move forward in the selection process. HISD found that only about 70 percent of those applicants passed the math test. Though the test was not technically included in the application process, this early screening tool provides an instructive example of the type of activity that can be embedded within an application form to weed out the unqualified candidates. If hiring for a math teacher or a science teacher, for example, you could add some very basic subject-related questions to their application forms to quickly weed out the worst candidates. Again, keep in mind that time saved *not* assessing poor candidates later in the selection process is time that you can use to better screen, and differentiate between, your much stronger candidates.

SUMMARY

While application forms have become somewhat of a dinosaur for many industries, there still remain many instances when they can be very helpful in the selection process. However, don't let them become an administrative burden; make sure you are getting useful information from them and, more importantly, that you can use them to narrow the focus of your search for the best candidates.

5

PREDICTING PERFORMANCE THROUGH WORK SAMPLES

Conventional wisdom suggests that the best predictor of future behavior is past behavior. The future behaviors we are trying to predict are called *criteria*, and they might include such outcomes as student learning, student satisfaction, effective parent-teacher relations, overall job performance, absenteeism, and turnover. However, we often don't have access to a candidate's past behavior to help us predict these criteria. Instead, we score a candidate's performance on selection tools to provide us with insight into how the candidate will likely perform on the job. Some assessments, such as personality tests, indicate the predisposition of an individual to act in a certain way but do not measure job behaviors directly. The scores on these assessments represent *indicators* of behavior, or signs.[1] A teaching candidate's score on the conscientiousness scale of a personality test would serve as an indicator of the candidate's potential for creating effective lesson plans on time. Presumably, creating and executing lesson plans in a timely manner would help the teacher succeed; the conscientiousness score, therefore, is an indicator of this job success criterion.

Although they are useful, indicators of predispositions for certain behaviors do not illustrate the candidate's performance or show us how the candidate will approach a task. For example, a teaching candidate scoring high on conscientiousness is predisposed to conscientiousness, but it is an inferential leap that this predisposition will translate to actual behaviors on the job, such as writing a viable lesson plan, sticking to the lesson plan, and maintaining a schedule.

A more direct way to predict job performance or other criteria is to sample work behaviors.[2] Work samples can be thought of as "miniaturized replicas of jobs."[3] The intention of these samples should be to "obtain measures that are as similar to the job criterion or criteria as possible."[4] Rather than relying on an indicator, such as a score on a conscientiousness test, candidates could provide samples of lesson plans that they have created or be asked to develop a lesson plan for a particular scenario.

By considering samples of the work rather than indicators of predispositions, the inference about what applicants are capable of doing and how they will perform is removed; sampling the work shows us the candidate's performance on the job criteria. The more features in common between the predictor and the job criterion, the greater the validity or the ability to predict the job criterion using work sample scores.[5] The more that the work sample tests replicate specific job criteria, such as defusing conflict with students, the greater the point-to-point relationship with the criteria. A review of eighty-five years of research on nineteen selection procedures found that work samples had the highest validity (.54) in predicting job performance, beyond assessments that measure indicators.[6] In a study of maintenance mechanics, for instance, work sample tests that were based on job tasks were more highly correlated with supervisors' ratings of job performance than were ability tests, such as the Test of Mechanical Comprehension.[7]

Job criteria can also be measured directly. Often these performance tests involve measuring such criteria as job performance during an internship, a tryout period, or a probationary period.[8] Candidates who do not perform adequately are terminated, and the selection process begins again. Job tryouts strongly predict job performance in entry-level jobs when training occurs after hiring (validity = .44).[9] But lengthy observations are neither cost nor time effective for teachers. We have found, however, that teaching simulations/work samples that can be scored objectively are relatively straightforward to build. Work samples predict job performance well in situations where applicants are already trained for the job.[10] They often can't be used with candidates unless they have received job-related experience or training, so if your population of candidates contains many first time teachers, you should take this into account when creating the work sample exercises. Candidates for teaching positions, for example, are trained through internships, structured student-teacher practica, and educational credentialing. Work samples used as selection methods will typically be especially relevant for predicting teacher performance, given that no additional job-relevant training is needed.

It is important to recognize that work samples vary in content. Unlike, say, a personality test, work samples are not subject to a prescribed set of assessment questions that constitute the definition for the construct (e.g., personality) being measured. Instead, work samples involve having the candidate complete essential job tasks as identified from a job analysis.[11] A job analysis is a formal study that identifies the major tasks involved in performing a specific job and the attributes required to successfully perform those tasks (see chapter 10). As a result, the content of work samples differs from job to job. To the extent that there is point-to-point comparison or behavioral consistency among the KSAOs measured in the work sample and the job criteria, validity will be enhanced.[12] For example, suppose a school leadership feels that effective teaching involves having teachers develop classroom games. A work sample in which candidates must create and test a classroom game would inform hiring committee members about which candidates likely would perform better on this portion of the job.

One issue to consider is the "bandwidth," or the "degree to which the entire job performance domain is represented by the tasks that make up" the work sample.[13] A representative sample of the job is needed for better validity, but practical issues must also be considered, such as how much time or financial resources are available for hiring new teachers. If few work sample exercises can be used, those few should focus on critical parts of the job.

Types of Work Samples

Although work sample content differs across jobs, work samples generally fall into distinct types or categories: realistic motor skills work samples (e.g., operating a sewing machine) and verbal work sample tests (e.g., solving language-oriented problems).[14] Although both types consist of sampled work from the job, the categories or format of the work samples help us predict different criteria. Researchers have found that motor skills work sample tests predicted job proficiency better than verbal work samples did, but the verbal work sample tests were better predictors of how well a candidate would do in training.[15] As such, if you are using work samples, it is important to include other predictors as well to ensure that a wider range of outcomes can be predicted.

Later, researchers expanded the list of work samples and identified four types: (1) psychomotor, (2) individual situational decision making, (3) job-related information, and (4) group discussion/decision making.[16] Psychomotor work samples require candidates to physically manipulate objects, such as creating a bulletin board welcoming new students. Individual situational decision-making calls for the candidate to respond to hypothetical situations. Candidates could be asked to respond to a scenario of an angry student exhibiting aggression by indicating how they would handle the situation. Job-related information samples tests applicants on job knowledge. An example of this would be having candidates complete written examinations of teaching principles and then submitting evidence of student success. Finally, group discussion/decision-making work samples require that candidates work together in discussing a topic. In the application stage, candidates might be asked to discuss curricula changes with each other and decide on a process for initiating changes.

Validity of Work Samples

Each type of work sample has demonstrated effectiveness in predicting performance outcomes. A review of more than sixty studies found that psychomotor and group discussion work samples best predicted performance as measured by supervisor ratings (validities of .44 and .35, respectively).[17] The psychomotor work samples also strongly predicted training performance

(.38) and how well the candidate later performed tasks on the job (.49). Job-related information strongly predicted training performance (.50), and situational decision making contributed the most to predicting job performance (.75) as measured by sampling employees' performance on work tasks. Each type of work sample predicted success for at least one criterion. Recently, however, researchers have pointed out methodological flaws in prior research. By reexamining data, they have estimated that the correlation between work sample tests and job performance approximate .33 rather than the higher validities reported in earlier research.[18] Despite the decrease in overall validity, it appears that work samples still predict job performance strongly and have other benefits as well, such as favorable applicant reactions and the potential for providing applicants with a job preview.

Of course, the extent to which work samples predict job performance depends on job tasks. For example, having candidates work together discussing a topic and making decisions might predict performance for a job requiring extensive teamwork but might have much lower value in predicting performance for teachers who maintain individual responsibility for many of their job requirements, such as planning lessons, delivering information, and assessing student performance. If your school emphasizes collaborative work or uses extensive team teaching, then these criteria would likely be very conducive to group discussion work samples. Other types of work samples, however, might better predict candidate success relevant to the more traditional teaching jobs. For example, a work sample in which raters observe the candidate teaching a class involves a psychomotor component and also tests job-related information. Practically speaking, in our experience, when we delineate and isolate tasks from other parts of the job, we undermine the real situation and the results distort predictions of job performance.[19] So, observing candidates engaged in the interactive tasks involved in teaching a class provides a sense of realism and makes for less distortion.

Validity of High-Fidelity Versus Low-Fidelity Work Samples/Job Simulations

How realistic should a work sample be to predict performance? Work samples differ on whether they are high fidelity (simulations that are realistic and require candidates to respond with task performance) or low fidelity (simulations that describe the task stimulus and call for candidates to provide a written or oral response).[20] Research has found low-fidelity simulations in which entry-level managerial candidates were presented with a situation and asked to choose their most and least likely responses correlated with supervisory ratings of performance (.28 to .37).[21] The validity of low-fidelity simulations for predicting performance has been found to be the same or slightly higher than high-fidelity simulations.[22] An alternative to the multiple-choice format is requiring respondents to explain verbally or in writing how they would react to scenarios.[23] The validity holds for this method, with a slight decrease, when offered in paper-and-pencil form.[24] Therefore, this type of simulation can be used in addition to other selection methods, like the interview, without incurring the additional expense of having to administer this work sample in a face-to-face format.[25] Situational decision making can be assessed relatively easily by school districts without the expense and time necessary for developing a high-fidelity simulation. For example, a multiple-choice test could be developed that presents a series of common scenarios. We have seen this done effectively with criteria such as parent relations, classroom management, and teaching struggling students. Not only can situational decision-making assessments be administered in a paper-and-pencil format, but they can be administered to a large group of candidates at one time, both reasons we have seen them eagerly adopted by schools that need to hire large numbers of teachers in a short period of time and with scarce resources.

It is tempting to consider these situational-based examples as analogous to knowledge tests or tests of predispositions rather than as work samples. Low-fidelity simulations usually build on existing knowledge to be seen as credible and realistic more so than the high-fidelity simulation.[26] In the low-fidelity work sample, however, candidates' responses represent criterion-relevant behavioral intentions more than actual indicators of job performance. They call forth procedural knowledge rather than declarative knowledge.[27] By asking candidates to consider a situation and choose the action they would consider taking, they likely recall how they behaved in similar situations or they extrapolate from situations with similar features. Therefore, their responses reflect their recollections of past behavior to predict future behavior.[28]

Teaching Portfolios

Similarly, we assess the past to predict the future when we evaluate teaching portfolios. Teaching portfolios constitute a work sample; they include examples from candidates' teaching experiences and can be considered a sample of job-related information. Portfolios differ from the common perceptions of work samples because they require candidates "to recount past endeavors or produce work products illustrative of (their) ability to perform across a variety of contexts."[29] They are not created on the spot in response to a situational question, nor are they the focus of a hands-on exercise. They reflect the knowledge that the candidate has gained and the outcomes she has attained through her structured experience. Rather than asking about experiences, the hiring committee benefits from evidence produced from situations the candidate has faced that are similar to those in the teaching job.

One question to consider is whether these portfolios and other work sample exercises measure candidates' typical performance or maximal performance relative to the job. Debate continues about whether work samples should measure how a candidate typically would act on the job or whether the exercises should capture the best a candidate can muster; however, some researchers suggest that if the purpose of the selection process is to hire candidates with the most potential, then measures of maximum performance might be more informative than measures of typical performance.[30] Portfolios likely include only the best examples of performance, but this might matter little for school districts choosing to hire teachers with the highest potential. Despite their promise for predicting performance, hiring committees rarely ask for portfolios from teaching candidates.[31] Fewer than half (44 percent) of twenty-eight administrators surveyed in one study listed the quality of the portfolio as "important" or "very important" in hiring decisions.[32] Similarly, another study found that principals rated the importance of candidates' portfolios or e-portfolios as substantially lower than other information presented in the application, such as verbal references, written references, and first impressions.[33] When using portfolio assessments, structured scoring is essential. The best teaching criteria to measure using portfolio assessment include lesson plans, customized student assessments, and video recordings of live teaching.

Teaching Samples

Interestingly, principals also tend to downplay the importance of other work sample tools, such as videos of instruction or demonstration lessons.[34] Applicants often do not provide videos or demonstration lessons as part of their application files. In addition, many online application processes limit the uploading of videos. More troubling, however, is that many of the surveyed principals doubted the validity of these work samples, despite what the personnel selection literature indicates about their potential for predicting job performance.[35] In our work, we have seen all matter of opinions on the utility of using teaching samples to predict teacher performance. We've worked with a network of schools that *never* observed the candidates teaching, and we've worked with an organization that would only accept applications from candidates who also submitted a five-minute videotaped teaching sample. When done right, teaching samples can be a wonderful opportunity to assess job-relevant criteria directly.

USING WORK SAMPLES/SIMULATIONS

Work samples function better as selection methods for well-defined jobs with relatively stable tasks; however, even loosely defined jobs can benefit from selection using work samples if the samples directly evaluate abilities that are needed for the job, such as using an in-box test to measure how a candidate responds to rapidly changing demands indicative of a dynamic job.[36] Differences in candidates might influence their work sample performance. In a study of military and civilian employees performing jobs of medium complexity, researchers found that work sample performance was strongly influenced by job knowledge and that job knowledge was influenced by job experience.[37] These results suggest that candidates with teaching experience or who have experienced extensive training opportunities in their educational programs likely will perform better on selection methods that measure job knowledge and that candidates with more job knowledge can parlay their knowledge into better performance on work sample methods. As a result, work samples may be less useful when a candidate pool contains a large number of first-time teachers. This is due, in part, to the fact that experienced teachers will have much more material from which to choose and can filter out the worst samples.

Applicants generally view work samples favorably.[38] They allow them to demonstrate their skills rather than answer questions that serve as an indicator of a predisposition. In addition, they provide a realistic job preview for candidates, giving them a good glimpse into the realities of the job and what they are getting into.[39] Work samples' strong link to job requirements emphasize their relevance to the job and render it less likely that unsuccessful applicants will lodge complaints that the test served as a poor proxy for the job.[40] Although rater observations often are used in rating work sample performance, the use of work samples helps eliminate rating biases or errors by forcing the raters to describe, rather than judge or evaluate, behaviors using a standardized form.[41] For example, suppose that a candidate for a teaching position is asked to engage in a role-play simulation of a conference with aggressive parents. Raters use a standardized form to record and describe the candidate's responses to the parents. The responses could then be compared to job-related responses indicating appropriate methods for dealing with aggression and conflict. In this manner, the simulation results should be evaluated consistently across candidates without individual raters' subjectivity or biases affecting the outcomes.

This is not to suggest that ratings are devoid of observation and judgment; both are required to assess performance on a work sample.[42] However, to the extent that assessors or raters lack reliability in their ratings, we can expect that our validity or accuracy in predicting criteria will erode. For example, in a study of aircraft mechanics, raters differed from each other in videotaped work sample performances. The researchers noted how the raters were often inaccurate in their observations, and the reasons for the variability in observations (e.g., experience) differed from those affecting how they judge or evaluate others (e.g., attention to detail).[43] However, other studies have found that accomplishment records and portfolios used as samples of teaching performance exhibit high reliability across raters.[44]

What to Measure with Work Samples

It is important to choose wisely which KSAOs to measure using work samples, as some are more easily measured with this technique than others. For teachers, a teaching sample is the most obvious choice. What better method to assess a teacher's ability than to watch him teach? Because a teaching observation is such a common and important type of work sample, we devote all of chapter 7 to it. Many other, not-so-obvious tasks that teachers perform on a daily basis are also well suited for work samples/simulations. When considering the types of tasks where performance is best suited for assessment through work samples, we have found that many soft skills are often well suited (e.g., communicating a difficult topic to a parent), as well as tasks that can be completed in a short period of time. As indicated in chapter 2, the following are a few of the types of soft skills we've seen measured:

- Professional communication: Demonstrates respect and courtesy when communicating with others
- Effective relationship building: Maintains effective working relationships with others
- Sensitivity to problems: Able to detect when something is likely to go wrong
- Respect for authority: Follows written and verbal directives from authority figures

Building Your Work Sample/Simulation

One of the best things about work samples is that you should be able to measure multiple KSAOs with each work sample. As such, you can design your work sample to be very cost effective by including many KSAOs within a single exercise. For this example, though, we keep it simple and focus on the first KSAO mentioned above: professional communication.

In our job analysis of a teacher's job at one school district, a task that received a very high importance rating was "Communicates effectively with parents (or guardians), teachers, counselors and administrators to resolve students' behavioral and academic problems." It's pretty clear that the skill "professional communication" directly relates to accomplishing this task. A method for assessing this skill would be to build a simulation in which a candidate must review some academic data on a child and then send an e-mail to that child's parents requesting a meeting to address and remedy their child's poor academic performance.

(Remember, this is a simple example; you can build your simulation out to measure a larger number of attributes if desired. For example, by giving the candidate raw data for this simulated student, you could add measuring the candidate's ability to "interpret academic data.") After the candidate composes the e-mail, you could simulate an angry e-mail reply from the parents in which they refuse to meet because of their busy work schedules. In asking the teacher candidate to reply back to this next step in the simulation, you're now measuring the candidate's skill at "building and maintaining effective relationships."

While principals and others within the school could develop this material, it should come from your best teachers. Whenever you build personnel selection content, you want to access a group of subject matter experts (SMEs). Your SMEs will help you make sure the content you create is highly relevant to effective performance on the job (that you are measuring KSAOs that predict performance on important tasks), appears valid to the candidates, and is scored accurately. In selecting a team of teacher SMEs, we typically look for the following characteristics in each member:

- Demonstrates an exemplary level of high performance as a teacher
- Holds at least a baccalaureate degree from an institution of higher education accredited by a recognized regional or national accrediting agency (master's degree preferred)
- Has at least five years of teaching experience

Other criteria for identifying SMEs may include teaching awards, peer nomination, and student feedback. The point is

98

to have your very best teachers serving as SMEs and helping you create your selection material.

Scoring Work Samples

SMEs can also help with the scoring rubric by determining what successful (and not-so-successful) performance would look like. What would the perfect e-mail requesting a meeting with the poor performing child's parents look like? What would a poorly constructed e-mail look like?

There are multiple ways to "score" this information:

- Form a focus group and ask the SMEs what the range of e-mails should look like (from exemplary to very poor)
- Ask for real examples. Ask SMEs to find e-mails that share similar characteristics with those in the simulation (e.g., reaching out to a parent to schedule a meeting over an uncomfortable topic)
- Put your SMEs to the test. Since these are your best teachers, ask them to write the e-mail themselves. This will help you with the exemplary rating on your scale, but you will likely have to use the focus group approach to gather the lowest rating

Figure 5.1 offers a sample of a scoring rubric for this sample simulation.

This simulation was intended to measure professional communication. We chose a five-point rating scale with three behavioral anchored ratings (BARs) to help better define the difference between each rating point. Some pros to using BARs are that they are behaviorally based and so they ensure higher

---

Figure 5.1

Sample scoring rubric for work samples/simulations

Candidate name: _____   Evaluator name: _____

Date: _____   School name: _____

Use the following table to score the work sample. Use the behavioral descriptions in each scale to help determine which rating is most appropriate for the applicant and then assign a rating to the criteria below. Remember that if a candidate does not rank at one of the extreme points (1 or 5) or the midpoint (3), you may use the 2 and 4 points of the rating scale.

Professional Communication				
1	2	3	4	5
Response lacks respectful manner. Response contains multiple grammatical errors. Response is neither clear nor concise.		Most of response is written in a respectful manner. One grammatical error was found in response. Most of response is written in clear and concise manner.		Response is written in a respectful manner. Proper grammar is used throughout response. Response is written in clear and concise manner.

reliability when applied consistently across multiple candidates. But BARs can be tedious and time consuming to create, so we devised them only for the midpoint (3) and extreme points (1 and 5) of the rating scale in our sample scoring sheet (see figure 5.1). By using a five-point scale, we allow the raters some freedom in scoring if, say, the candidate does not quite meet the 5 but does exceed the 3. If measuring multiple KSAOs, separate rating scales and BARs would have to be developed for each KSAO. The ratings for each KSAO could then be aggregated into an overall score for each candidate, who could then be rank-ordered and compared based on the overall score (see chapter 8 for more on comparing applicants).

SUMMARY

Though they can be time consuming to build and implement, work samples/simulations are powerful tools for assessing a candidate's ability to perform specific aspects of a job based on the premise that the best predictor of future behavior is past behavior. Instead of assessing a candidate's predisposition to behave in a certain manner, we can measure the job criteria directly. Work samples have the added benefit of being able to assess multiple criteria, which can help offset the time and expense involved in building them. They also provide strong predictive validity, and candidate reactions are typically quite positive, since they can provide an effective means for communicating a realistic job preview.

6

ADDING STRUCTURE
TO INTERVIEWS

The hiring process for almost all jobs includes at least one interview as a selection method.[1] Teacher selection is no exception. Most hiring teams responsible for screening teaching candidates consider the interview to be the most important aspect of the hiring process.[2] This confidence in the interview appears well founded, though research in this area makes clear that not all interviews are created equal. Meta-analytic research finds that candidates' interview results have a mean validity of .37 for predicting job performance and a mean validity of .36 for predicting training performance.[3] Although these validity coefficients are strong, different types and formats of interviews vary in how well they help organizations predict which candidates will emerge as effective employees.

INTERVIEW TYPES

Interviews differ in the types of information they collect. Situational interviews (SIs) include questions that describe a scenario and call for candidates to predict how they would respond to the situation.[4] For example, if maintaining effective relationships with parents or guardians constitutes an important component of the teacher's job, interviewers might describe a situation to candidates in which parents are upset because their child is performing poorly: the child has told her parents that the teacher is grading her unfairly and is picking on her; the parents arrive at a scheduled parent-teacher conference behaving aggressively and confront the teacher with their child's allegations. The interviewers then ask the candidate to discuss how he would handle this situation.

Behavior description interviews (BDIs) are similar in that they describe a situation but differ by asking the candidates how they addressed the situation in the past.[5] This type of interview uses recollections of past behavior to predict future behavior. Although this type of interview elicits candidates' responses through the use of scenarios, the focus on candidates' experience leads researchers to consider the behavioral interview as a form of job-related interview.[6] Job-related interviews are experience based. The questions focus on past experience in job-related areas but are not situational in nature.[7] If the job of teacher requires effective use of conflict resolution techniques, a sample job-related interview question might ask: "Tell us about a time when you resolved conflict between you and another person. What did you do? What could you have done differently?" Psychological interviews, which are generally conducted by a psychologist, include questions that are designed to elicit information about personal traits, such as conscientiousness or agreeableness.[8]

SIs and BDIs show strong validity in predicting job performance. For example, SI questions showed a validity of .46 when used with hourly workers and a validity of .30 when used with foremen.[9] Validity estimates for BDI questions tend to be slightly higher than validity estimates for SI questions. Compared to the validity of an unstructured interview (.07), BDI questions yielded a validity of .54 in a student sample.[10] In a study of pulp mill employees, BDI (past-oriented) questions correlated .51 with job performance and SI (future-oriented) questions correlated .39 with performance.[11] Past-oriented questions provided more information about job performance even after accounting for scores on the future-oriented questions and other test scores. One possibility for differences in how well these interviews predict performance rests with the complexity of the job. A meta-analysis of existing research found that situational interviews had lower validity (.30) in predicting job performance in highly complex jobs than in jobs with lower complexity.[12] BDIs maintained high validity for predicting performance in complex jobs (.51). The researchers suggest that possible reasons for the lower SI validities could be difficulties constructing situational questions for highly complex work and assessing complex responses and the possibility that candidates report what they think the interviewers want to hear rather than what they would actually do in the situation. These findings seem especially important for the complex job of teacher.

Despite their differing validities, it is important to realize that SIs and BDIs both serve as valid predictors and that job seekers tend to view selection decisions more positively when SI questions are used rather than unstructured interviews.[13] Thus, districts may need to choose between the best predictive validity (BDI format) and the most positive applicant reactions (SI format). While validity is generally the paramount concern when selecting candidates, practical circumstances could dictate that applicant reaction may need to be a greater consideration. For example, when the applicant pool is small relative to the number of open positions, it becomes more important to prevent applicant attrition due to a negative experience with the hiring process. In this case, it may be worth sacrificing some validity in order to enhance the applicant experience.

Job-related and psychological interviews also show validity for predicting performance, but typically their validity coefficients are smaller than those of SIs and BDIs. According to meta-analytic results, job-related interviews correlated .28 with performance, and psychological interviews correlated .20.[14] Thus, information that is better for predicting performance is more likely gained through the use of SIs or BDIs.

STRUCTURED VERSUS UNSTRUCTURED INTERVIEWING

Interviews differ in the amount of structure included in the instrument and throughout the process. Adding structure increases standardization and helps interviewers know which questions to ask and how to evaluate responses.[15] Most interviews, even structured ones, contain an unstandardized part at the beginning that includes small talk designed to put candidates at ease. Interviewers react positively to candidates who build rapport with them; these candidates are rated higher on the subsequent interview questions and are more likely to receive job offers.[16] The initial evaluations reflect competency assessments, not just liking and similarity, and the candidate's verbal skill and level of extroversion affect her ability to convey this positive impression, whether or not these qualities relate to the job.[17] In fact, one study summarizing research in the field found that while job-related interview content correlates with interview ratings, interviewee performance (social skills) has a stronger relationship with interview ratings.[18] This suggests the need for structure in the interview. But what happens when an entire interview is unstructured?

Suppose that a school district reviews applications and work sample scores to narrow its applicant pool. The district invites the strongest candidates to an interview. Each candidate is asked interview questions that are unique to that candidate. Even if two candidates are asked the same question, follow-up questions differ, and the responses are not scored the same, or perhaps no score is used to indicate the quality of the candidate's responses. How easy would it be to choose the best candidate from among those interviewed?

Without structure in the interview, biases can creep into the decision-making process. We might ask interesting questions (e.g., "What do you like to do in your spare time?"), but some of the questions are not related to the job and could elicit responses from candidates that, if used in hiring decisions, could result in discrimination against protected classes. We obtain ample interesting information about the candidate but find it difficult to sift through it for meaningful data related to the job. Further, when we find such data, we are unable to compare responses across candidates because we asked each candidate different questions. Despite our approach to using an interview as a means for identifying the best candidate for the job, the complexity of selecting the right person became even greater with our use of an unstructured interviewing process. Not surprisingly, the validity of unstructured interviews is relatively low.[19] Given the time and expense of interviewing candidates, districts benefit more from using a more structured approach to interviewing because structured interviews will have higher validity for predicting teacher success.

This scenario describes an entirely unstructured approach to interviewing. More realistically, interviews vary as to how structured they are. Researchers have identified fifteen structural components that influence the content of the interview and the evaluation process.[20]

Content components impact the type of information interviewers gain from the interview. The seven content components include:

- Using a job analysis
- Asking the same questions of all candidates
- Limiting prompting
- Using better questions
- Conducting a longer interview
- Controlling ancillary information
- Discouraging unique questions posed by the candidates

Evaluation components affect the process used to judge responses and make decisions about the candidates. The eight evaluation components include:

- Rating each answer or using multiple scales
- Using anchored rating scales (BARs)
- Having interviewers take detailed notes during the interview
- Using multiple interviewers
- Using the same interviewers across candidates
- Allowing no discussion between interviews
- Training the interviewers
- Calculating interview scores for statistical prediction instead of using clinical prediction, or "gut feelings," for making decisions

If these guidelines are followed, highly structured interviews will predict job performance in a wide range of jobs much better than unstructured interviews. One study showed that a structured interview for hiring entry-level production employees had a corrected validity coefficient of .56 for predicting performance.[21] In our own research, we have found statistically significant uncorrected validity coefficients above .30 for the interview components of teacher selection processes.[22]

IMPROVING INTERVIEWS THROUGH STRUCTURE
Conduct a Job Analysis

Structured interviews are based on job requirements.[23] Interview responses are only useful if they help predict how well someone will perform the job. As discussed in chapter 5, behavioral consistency between a selection method and the job often establishes the validity of the selection method.[24] Unlike physical work samples, interviews do not call for candidates to perform motor tasks; however, situational or behavioral interviews measure the quality of candidates' responses when they indicate how they would handle given scenarios (SIs) or how they have handled situations in the past (BDIs).

Given that interview questions describe a candidate's behavior during various job tasks, they presumably measure some aspects of the knowledge, skills, abilities, and other characteristics (KSAOs) needed to perform the job. It is particularly important in an interview to stay focused on job-relevant KSAOs and not let the conversations with candidates wander into non-job-related issues, such as whether certain professors still teach at the state university, what hobbies the candidate pursues, or which football teams are most likely to play in a bowl game. These superfluous questions do not provide the interviewer with valid information and are more likely to distract her attention from the task at hand and may even trigger some bias that could influence her judgment.

To illustrate the use of job analysis in question development, suppose we are developing an interview protocol for a school district and notice from the list of KSAOs in our job analysis that one essential task is to "prepare and implement remedial programs to support students requiring extra help." (If this item does not show up in your job analysis, you may need to go back to the drawing board or locate some new SMEs.) Teachers who perform this task must have knowledge of the subject matter, knowledge of curriculum and program design, and the ability to identify struggling students. The district develops an interview question that measures the candidate's approach for assessing students and identifying those who are struggling and for developing and implementing a program that will help the students master the subject matter without being stigmatized. For example, we might ask a candidate for a math teacher position: "Put yourself in this scenario: You have introduced fractions to your class and you sense that some students are struggling with the concepts. Others are catching on quickly. You know the students must master fractions before moving to more complex material. How will you address this issue?" By asking this same question of all candidates, you ensure a reliable measurement on which all candidates can be compared. By using a structured, as opposed to unstructured, question, you also increase validity in your decisions. From the candidates' perspective, the use of this type of question increases the chances that they will feel the hiring process was fair, as compared to being asked an unstructured question like "What is your greatest strength?" or "What do you like most about teaching?" And for those candidates who may not have much teaching experience, they will benefit from these kinds of job-related questions because they provide a realistic preview to likely scenarios they will face should they be selected. In some cases, these kinds of questions can be used to help poor-fitting candidates to self-select out of the hiring process. We've seen this when hiring teachers for schools with particularly challenging students. It is far better for a candidate to know what the job will be like and to pull herself out of the applicant pool than to be surprised when she arrives on the job.

Developing questions based on KSAOs requires the use of SMEs who can use their familiarity with the job to devise face valid questions that stick to the job analysis. Ideally, three questions should be drafted for every one question you hope to retain. Thus, if you are trying to make an interview with 12 questions cover four different KSAOs, you should have the SMEs draft 36 initial questions. The draft questions should include some indication of a range of expected answers. For instance, detailed anchors could be written for the worst, best, and mid-range responses. SMEs should evaluate these draft questions by having them link each question to the intended KSAOs in a blind matching process. The questions that a majority of SMEs agree best address each KSAO can be included. If your initial drafts are of high enough quality, this process may result in enough KSAO-linked questions to allow for multiple forms of the interview (providing added security) or can provide a re-serve of questions to turn to if your validation research or in-terviewer feedback during piloting shows that some questions don't work as well as originally anticipated.

Choose Question Types That Contain Structure

Situational, behavioral, and job-related questions contain more structure than psychological or open-ended questions that measure traits, goals, or attitudes, which lack clear bound-aries or details that could allow applicant faking and are am-biguous enough to obscure their link with job performance.[25] Given that interviewers' initial impressions of candidates affect interview scores, it is necessary to use highly structured ques-tions rather than trait-based questions to mitigate this carry-over effect.[26]

Interestingly, many school districts currently assess such traits in the interview. For example, a sample of Wisconsin K–12 principals reported using the interview to measure per-sonal characteristics more so than professional attributes.[27] One-fourth of the sixty Wisconsin respondents used the inter-view to gauge positive attributes of excitement, and 20 percent assessed appearance and confidence. When asked what nega-tive attributes they measured using the interview, respondents again pointed to personal characteristics, such as poor appearance (32 percent), poor preparation (13 percent), and arrogance (12 percent). They did use interviews to gauge professional attributes of content knowledge and the extent to which interview responses were appropriately detailed, but most of the focus in the interview was on their assessment of personal characteristics. It is important to note that these findings do not suggest that the principals failed to assess professional qualifications altogether; they may have examined professional characteristics earlier in the selection process as a means for narrowing the interview pool to qualified candidates.[28] Researchers identified similar results with decentralized Florida school districts, where principals, who served as interviewers in the twenty-minute interviews, primarily attended to candidates' personal characteristics (e.g., enthusiasm, communication ability, body language).[29]

Other researchers have remarked on teacher interviews shifting from a method used for assessing subject matter knowledge or teaching skills to a way for districts to assess teachers' educational beliefs, attitudes, and values.[30] In an evaluation of one such commercially available off-the-shelf interview, researchers found that the interview predicted performance better for secondary teachers than for elementary teachers; they suggested that the interview may have been unstable in predicting different grade levels because different beliefs, attitudes, and values were needed for success at these varying grade levels. While they called for more research in this area, their data does show a stronger correlation between candidates' responses and administrator ratings of the candidates than with other criteria, such as student success. This study suggests that these values-based questions might be less helpful for school districts in predicting teacher success than methods with a more direct link to job content. However, other researchers posit that principals primarily use interviews as a measure of personality, as a means for filling voids in skill, and to "ensure that teacher candidates fit the cultural norms and values of the school as an organization."[31] They contend that teacher effectiveness lacks consistency in definition; therefore, it will be "difficult to advocate for specific tools and processes over others."[32]

While we agree that defining teacher success is not a one-size-fits-all proposition, we strongly encourage schools to take the time to define teaching success at a local level and use this definition to drive their hiring process. As such, after doing a job analysis, it may be important to consider personal characteristics, such as a candidate's attitude about education and learning in the context of a given school. For instance, if a school has a recent history of exceptional performance, where all students achieve above benchmarks, a principal may seek out teachers who have a strong belief in strengths-based education to help their students hone their skills and focus on a subset of their many talents. But a school with a recent history of fewer than 30 percent of students meeting state standards on verbal and math skills may need to assess teachers' resilience levels to ensure that they won't give up on their students. Keep in mind that although assessing traits may be legitimate for a given situation, this doesn't mean that the interview questions cannot be structured in some way. For example, candidates' attitudes might be measured by evaluating their priorities and plans for addressing an issue posed in a situational question.

Use the Same Questions

One of the simplest yet most powerful design principles to follow when structuring interviews is to use the same set of questions for all candidates who are being considered for a given job. Interviewers often find it difficult to compare interview results when candidates have answered different questions. A structured approach involves presenting all candidates with the same questions in the same order, with deviations allowed only to provide flexibility in gathering more information related to the job.[33] Using prompts or follow-up questions might introduce biasing information or irrelevant data, since only some candidates may be prompted. Interviewers who use standardized prompting questions reduce the likelihood of gathering information inconsistently across candidates.

For example, teachers must often work with others as part of a team to accomplish objectives for the school or the district. We might measure the candidate's approach to teamwork by asking the main question: "Tell us about a time when you worked as part of a team." We could then prompt the candidate for detailed information relevant to the job, such as, "Describe to us what made your team (in)effective. What was your role on the team? What could you have done to make the team function more effectively?" Interviewers who use the standardized prompts gain information that can then be compared across candidates for decision making. But if prompts are unstructured and vary by candidate, then interviewers will have different information for each candidate, and it will be difficult to compare them when making the hiring decision. In this example, one candidate may be asked as a follow-up, "Who formed the team and how were you chosen?" (which isn't about teamwork at all), while another may be asked, "Did you enjoy being on the team?" (which could get at a candidate's characteristics but may not be relevant to their ability to work well in a team environment). The results of these two sample follow-ups may lead one candidate to be perceived as a superstar (perhaps the answer was something like, "I was chosen because the principal knew I would make sure the job got done, even if others didn't follow through"). The second question may lead interviewers to think the person has a "bad attitude" (perhaps the answer indicated she didn't like being on teams because she had experienced several instances when one or more members became overly bossy). In this case, the candidates cannot be compared equitably because the interviewers do not have comparable information about each.

Sample the Content Domain

Your district is hiring new teachers and you are developing the interview portion of the selection process. How many interview questions, or items, should you include? Think about each question as a sample of the candidate's knowledge, response, or behavior. The more samples you have, the more confidence you will have in your assessment of the candidate.

Think about how you judge a new restaurant. Before you make an overall assessment of the restaurant, you sample a few items from the menu; without sampling a representative portion of the menu, your opinion could be swayed by the quality of just one menu item. Perhaps you try a dessert that is exceptional and a mediocre entrée but overlook the appetizers entirely. How much can you really say about the restaurant as a whole? Not much.

Similarly, you must take enough samples of a candidate's interview responses to make a realistic evaluation of his capabilities on the KSAO being measured. Suppose you ask the candidate three questions related to teaching high school math classes as a means for assessing content knowledge of tenth grade math. If the candidate performs poorly on one question but excels on the other two, does this mean she fails the interview, at most earning a 66 percent? Do you have enough questions to get a clear picture of the candidate's knowledge? Longer interviews likely will provide a more reliable result because of the larger number of items used to measure; however, longer interviews might fatigue candidates and interviewers. A review of the literature suggests that interviews probably should not exceed one hour; two-thirds of interviews last between 30 and 60 minutes in length, with half of the interviews containing 15 to 20 questions.[34] This highlights another advantage to using structured interview questions: because there is a clear focus on specific information being sought, candidates don't tend to ramble on wondering when to stop talking. As such, they can be much faster to ask and answer, which should result in more items and a more reliable measure.

Stick with the Right Information, Not Necessarily More Information

In terms of questions to include, interviewers who focus on essential functions of the job end up collecting information that has a much stronger likelihood of predicting whether or not the candidates will perform effectively on the job. However, counter to our previous assertion of the value of lengthening the interview time, gaining additional information above the sixty-minute mark doesn't always provide better prediction. What matters more than the volume of information is the quality of the data collected. In some cases, interviewers can be distracted during the interview by other sources of information, such as applications, resumes, or test scores. When interviewers spend time verifying information or having candidates provide detail from these ancillary sources, they tend not to dedicate enough time to gathering unique information using the interview itself. If this distracting information is considered for some, but not all, candidates, the resulting interview scores could be unreliable; in addition, the interview score might include consideration of these ancillary sources, essentially counting the sources twice for some candidates and only once for others.[35] Application forms, resumes, and other sources of data representing selection methods outside the interview should be scored separately unless structured interview questions and scoring rubrics are specifically developed and used with each candidate in order to glean more job-relevant details about past performance, credentials, or experience.

Allowing candidates to ask questions throughout the interview introduces yet another source of unreliability and potentially undermines the validity of the interview.[36] Understandably, candidates often have questions about the job during the interview; however, allowing candidates to ask their questions interrupts the question flow, takes time away from asking relevant questions, and undermines standardization. These types of questions may also allow candidates to steer the interview and affect the extent to which results can be compared from one candidate to the next. To avoid these problems, interviewers should allow candidates to ask only clarifying questions and alert candidates at the beginning of the interview that there will be time afterward to respond to questions. You may also offer candidates the opportunity to schedule a nonevaluative follow-up interview just for responding to questions or specifically ask for questions and then score them as a measure of how well the candidate prepared for the interview.

Score Interview Responses for Individual Questions and Use Anchored Rating Scales

Interviews generate a wealth of information. So after collecting the interviews, the important question becomes about how best to use all the information. If interviewers read their notes, they might form a general impression of each applicant; however, what would prevent one interviewer from homing in on a response to a specific question and allowing that single response to overly influence her overall assessment? And what if another interviewer focuses his overall assessment almost exclusively on the response to a different question? This variability does little for helping interviewers evaluate candidates against job-relevant criteria. A solution for making sense of the large volume of qualitative data from interviews is to compare candidates' responses using standardized rating scales, or rating rubrics. Standardized rating scales can be created for each question, for multiple questions that comprise a dimension such as "teamwork," or for all questions combined at the end of the interview.[37] If only certain questions are posed to all candidates, each interviewer should generate a score for each question. In this way, cross-candidate comparisons are made easily based on the same set of responses. Nonstructured qualitative data, such as side notes or off-handed comments and observations ("Did you notice that he looked a lot like our former principal?"), while interesting, fail in furthering efficient comparisons of candidates. Instead, interviewers need to apply a standardized scoring system to all qualitative information so that they can consistently assign ratings for each response and thus give each candidate an equal chance to succeed at the interview.

While interview questions can vary in the extent to which they are structured, so too can rating scales for evaluating candidate responses vary in their structure.[38] Some rating scales include examples or anchors that illustrate high-, medium-, and low-quality answers. Others include generic descriptions at each extreme (e.g., "Addressed emotional responses first and then identified tasks needed to be completed") or general evaluations (e.g., "Excellent response"). Behavioral anchored rating scales (BARs) are popular and are viewed positively by interviewers and candidates.[39] In chapter 5 we talked about how to use SMEs to create BARs for scoring work samples/simulations. SMEs can be used in the same manner to create BARs for scoring your interview questions. As with scoring work samples, when SMEs participate in creating BARs, it is important to pilot the rating scale anchors so that the rating scales can be used efficiently and accurately by interviewers. Likewise, if practical, interviewers should be trained to ensure inter-rater reliability when rating candidate responses.

Document Responses

Suppose a hiring team conducts an interview of three candidates in a row. The interviewers meet two days after the interviews to discuss the candidates in more depth. Unfortunately, none of the interviewers took detailed notes; they simply jotted down their evaluations (or worse, just their overall impressions) at the end of the interview. One interviewer commented on one candidate, "Seems nervous, answers were not always complete, impulsive." Another wrote only "not a good hire" about one, and the third focused his notes primarily on the candidates' tenures at prior jobs and educational backgrounds. Without more detailed notes about responses to each question, the interviewers now find themselves struggling to remember what the candidates said and which candidates provided the best answers on specific items. They would have benefited from taking more extensive notes for each question as the interview progressed.

It is particularly important when taking notes that the notes focus on each answer independently, so that the interviewers are not forming judgments about the overall viability of the candidate. Each question should be designed to provide information about a job-related KSAO; and when combined, the scores can be used to judge a candidate's overall viability. Although it has been difficult to pinpoint the effects note taking have on the validity of the interview, it is likely that taking notes has accommodated our limitations in processing information, so it likely improves the quantity and quality of information we consider later when evaluating applicants.[40]

Use the Same Interviewer(s)

Using the same interviewer(s) across candidates adds structure to the interview process and increases validity.[41] The same interviewers assess the candidates consistently, whereas substituting interviewers can mean that responses are documented or evaluated differently, especially if other parts of the interview process are unstructured (e.g., no note-taking requirement, rating scales with very general anchors). Using different interviewers also introduces random error into judgments about candidates. "Different interviewers ask different questions and evaluate answers differently."[42] When this happens, differences between two candidates' scores on a particular interview question could reflect more about the differences between interviewers than differences between candidates.

Say that a school district is interviewing a handful of candidates for a job opening at the last possible moment. Due to schedule conflicts, not all interviewers can be present at all interviews.

While there is a practical need that will almost certainly result in the interviews being conducted with a different group of interviewers, it is important to recognize the trade-offs of making such a choice. A few strategies can be employed to compensate for the loss in reliability when different raters are used:

- Train interviewers so their ratings are likely to be similar when the same response is given
- Use a high level of structure on other components of the interview to minimize interviewer effects
- Select and include only the most effective interviewers (such as those with direct job knowledge)[43]

Organizations can actually use multiple interviewers as a way to increase the structure of interviews and to decrease the potential for bias.[44] This could mean that interviewers serve on a panel to interview the candidate at the same time or that they interview the candidate individually in a serial manner. Although studies have found that panels predict job performance better than serial individual interviews, some research has found that using a panel interview can actually decrease validity, possibly because candidates find it intimidating to interview with multiple people at once.[45] Research within school districts indicates that using hiring teams as panel interviewers is a popular practice. The composition of hiring teams differs quite a bit from district to district.

In one study of sixty principals responsible for K–12 hiring, those who used a hiring panel approach were almost always involved in the interview themselves. Most respondents (55 percent) stated that content or grade-level teachers participate in the interview, and almost half (42 percent) involve additional teachers. Nearly all districts use a decentralized team-based approach when interviewing candidates for teacher positions, with teams used to interview candidates 92 percent of the time.[46] Other research indicates that team interview composition may be more flexible in some districts, with teams comprised of a convenient grouping of teachers, a representative sample of teachers across various categories, teachers from a particular grade level, or teachers from a specific academic department.[47] In a group of Florida school districts where principals are not actively involved in interviewing, the principals still retain a connection to the process by being introduced by the team to promising candidates. The team approach is also often used by principals to assess the fit between the candidates and different groups with whom they would likely work on a regular basis, such as grade-level colleagues, subject matter department heads, or school administrators.

One of the fundamental advantages to using groups of interviewers is that the district can collect multiple ratings of a single candidate in one sitting. If not handled properly, however, it is very easy to undermine the data interviewers collect. Hiring managers need to use caution when using interview panels to avoid potential data contamination between interviewers. For example, suppose a hiring team is interviewing multiple candidates in one day. Team members go to lunch between interviews, and over coffee their conversation turns to how candidates performed during the morning interviews. These conversations potentially undermine a structural component of the interview: if interviewers discuss irrelevant information or begin changing their standards, the validity of their assessments could be compromised.[48] Only once the interviews are complete and interviewers finish their individual ratings should the team come together to discuss candidate performance. This doesn't mean interviewers can't share a meal, just that they should complete their ratings independently and that they should focus the conversation away from the candidates. Not unlike jury deliberations in a legal proceeding, it may help before and during the interview process to provide interviewers with specific guidance about when it is appropriate to discuss the candidates.

Train Interviewers

Training interviewers introduces them to the questions and teaches them how to use follow-up prompts, take notes, and make ratings. In some cases, training calibrates the interviewers so that they rate the same responses reliably in comparison to each other (referred to as inter-rater reliability). We've seen districts devote as much as three full days to establishing inter-rater reliability among interviewers in an attempt to ensure accuracy of ratings and comparability of scores across candidates. Some researchers have suggested that the more unstructured the interview, the more training will be needed, and the more structured the interview, the less training will be required.[49] One meta-analysis of more than 18,000 interview studies found that interviewer training significantly improves validity of decisions made from interviews, regardless of whether the interview itself is structured.[50]

While training interviewers is an important part of the hiring process and training can improve accuracy, what works at one district may not work at another. For school districts considering interviewer training, the costs of training may need to be weighed against the costs of structuring interviews. If your resources are limited, it could be that creating structure in the interview process is a better investment than using unstructured interviews and training interviewers on effective interviewing skills. Another option is to direct most of your effort on improving the interview itself by creating a simpler training program. For example, interview training can be used to familiarize the interviewers with the structured interview process and how to use it correctly, rather than the more elaborate training that involves standardizing the interviewers judgments (inter-rater reliability), as would be needed with an unstructured interview process. In the best case, interviews should be structured and interviews should be trained.

Combine Scores Statistically Rather Than Intuitively

Most interviews are scored by having interviewers use either consensus or statistical rules (e.g., averaging, summing) to combine their ratings into total scores.[51] Using intuition, or an interviewer's global impression, yields less structure and could reflect irrelevant information—and, again, different interviewers might consider different dimensions to be more or less important. The best method for scoring interviews is for interviewers to follow a structured process for reaching consensus on each candidate. To do this, each interviewer shares his or her rating on the first question. When there is a significant disagreement in the ratings (e.g., more than one point difference on a five-point scale), interviewers discuss why they made their ratings and come to an agreement about what the final rating should be. While building consensus might include some subjectivity, during the dialogue about each candidate, interviewers have an opportunity to challenge each others' interpretations, perceptions, or biases, and the discussion often leads to more valid assessments of future performance.[52] When there is only small disagreement (e.g., a rating of 3 versus a 4 on a five-point scale), then simply averaging the ratings should suffice.

Prevalence in the Schools

Principals and other interviewers who are not familiar with structured interviews often resist them when they're first introduced. Gregarious types (common among principals) who prefer to chat with candidates and socialize during an interview will find it difficult to "get to know" someone during a structured interview. In many ways that is the point. Structure prevents people from forming quick, irrational, general opinions that are so commonly formed in social settings. The very things that make structured interviews effective at predicting future performance make them feel awkward to administer.

Despite the early difficulties of introducing these tools, many schools have come to see the advantages. A survey of 300 urban and rural principals across multiple levels (elementary, middle, and high schools) revealed that school districts do use many interview best practices.[53] Specifically, respondents reported using structured interviews that posed the same questions across candidates, taking notes, preparing questions in advance, focusing on situational and behavior-based questions, using multiple interviewers, and using a rubric with anchored rating scales to evaluate the interview responses. Principals who had received interviewer training were significantly more likely to use a standardized rubric than those with no training. Thus, it appears that many school districts may have already introduced important elements of structure into their interview processes. As researchers have noted, "There is no good rationale for using completely unstructured interviews."[54] While the structured interview may be increasingly common among school districts, hiring managers would do well to recognize that the more structured the interviews are, the more accurately candidate performance will predict future job performance. Thus, even if you currently use a structured interview system, it may be useful to review each of the fifteen dimensions of structure detailed previously to see where your system excels and where it could be improved.

INTERVIEWING INDIVIDUAL CANDIDATES VERSUS GROUPS OF CANDIDATES

A number of organizations capitalize on the efficiency of conducting interviews with groups of candidates instead of interviewing each candidate separately. In group interviews, multiple candidates form a sort of panel, and each is asked to answer the interviewers' questions. Candidates hear each others' answers, and candidates who go last have the opportunity to observe the reactions of interviewers to prior candidates' responses. Despite the cost savings, group interviews present potential problems. Interviewees perceive the group interview as less fair than individual interviews.[55] Furthermore, interviewees are more likely to borrow responses from earlier respondents. Additionally, ratings made of candidates during group interviews are not as accurate at predicting outcomes as the ratings made in one-on-one interviews. Although these results stem from research with undergraduate students and not employees with more at stake, they suggest caution in trying to gain selection information in a group format.

Group interviews have been used successfully, however, for hiring hospitality employees, in which participants who have applied for different positions and have varied backgrounds are assigned to groups, and so the interview serves as an opportunity to observe group dynamics and the extent to which applicants work with others.[56] This particular interview method points out the need to consider the job; the interview format will be more valid for predicting outcomes when it coincides with job requirements. If we are hiring individuals to work together and form teams, as in the hospitality field, a group interview might tell us much about their potential to work together. When hiring teachers, however, group interviews are likely to be less valid predictors in part because team behavior is typically a smaller part of the teaching job. If a group interview method is used to hire teachers, the link back to the job should be clear, scoring procedures should be very structured, interviewers should be trained regarding managing their reactions, and validity research (should be conducted to ensure the accuracy of the results for predicting teaching success (see chapter 9).

PHONE INTERVIEW—MAKE OR BREAK CHARACTERISTICS

Interviews conducted by telephone can be highly efficient because they decrease cost associated with travel and room arrangements and require far less of a commitment from candidates than in-person interviews. Telephone interviews are often used by school districts to screen candidates on specific requirements prior to scheduling them for on-site visits (e.g., subject knowledge, school location, teaching schedule, etc.).

Although many phone interviews are conducted in the early stages of selection as prescreening for early decisions, or to see if candidates will be invited on-site for further assessment, some schools conduct the primary selection interview over the telephone. Importantly, phone interviews seem to be just as effective at predicting future job performance as in-person interviews. One company hiring salespeople found that a behavior-based interview administered by telephone predicted performance in five key areas as well as likely turnover within twenty-nine months.[57] As such, it is important to consider reliability and validity when designing the content and scoring of phone interviews, just as you would with a live interview.

Although telephone interviews can provide valid inferences about a candidate's capabilities on the job, some research suggests that telephone interviews and face-to-face interviews may differ in substantive ways. For example, one study found that interviewers using semi-structured phone interviews were less likely to participate with the interviewee in completing the interviewee's thoughts and less likely to provide vocal acknowledgments (e.g., "Yes, I see)," perhaps because of the need to listen carefully to what is being said in the absence of nonverbal cues.[58] These authors found that interviews conducted by phone ended sooner than those conducted in person. Also, interviewees more often asked for clarification, if needed, during questioning and checked with the interviewer regarding the adequacy of their responses.

One study of MBA students engaging in mock interviews documented that interviewers evaluated telephone-interviewed applicants more favorably than they did those interviewed in person. The researchers speculated that the absence of less favorable visual cues or the need for applicants to be more animated to make up for missing nonverbal cues could account for these results.[59] Applicants did not differ in their opinion of the telephone interview as compared with the face-to-face interview, building on prior findings that these interview types do not differ substantively on how fair or just they appear to be.[60]

However, this finding does not appear to be stable across studies. In one study of applicant reactions to interview methods, researchers interviewed and surveyed 802 applicants. Those interviewed by telephone viewed the interview as significantly less fair than those interviewed in person, and they were less likely to say they would accept a job offer from the organization.[61] This finding may differ depending on applicant personality. The preference for in-person interviews was especially strong for individuals who were high self-monitors. (Self-monitoring is a personal characteristic that involves being concerned with how one is perceived by others.) Self-monitors will quickly adapt their behavior in order to fit different situations. During phone interviews, these individuals could not interpret cues from telephone interviews in order to tailor their behavior.

Research supports the validity of telephone interviewing, with some cautions apparent from the inconsistent results. As an initial screen early in the selection process, the decreased cost of interviewing by telephone could compensate for potential negative perceptions, especially for school districts conducting their spring hiring, with large batches of applications needing to be processed in a short period. Effective screening initially makes it more viable for the school district to meet with smaller numbers of candidates later in the selection process for face-to-face interaction.

STRUCTURED INTERVIEW SCORING

There is plenty of evidence that interviewers have a difficult time remaining objective during the interview process—no matter how determined they may be to do so. In one study, where principals served as the interviewers, the principals generated quick impressions about job suitability quickly; 19 percent indicated that they knew whether the applicant was suited to the job within the first five minutes ("I could just tell"). Not only had these principals decided quickly, but they were making global decisions rather than looking at the many facets of a candidate's qualification. In the study, other principals took longer to decide about candidates, with 58 percent of principals indicating that they had made a global decision about suitability for the job by the end of the first interview. Interestingly, 19 percent stated that they never really trusted their own assessments of job suitability until the teachers were actually on the job.[62] These findings are consistent with research on how initial impressions predict interview outcomes and job offers.[63] It is unclear to what extent these evaluations have validity, but interviewers do seem to frequently judge competence early in the process, using information that goes beyond just "liking" and similarity; candidate extroversion and verbal skills engender positive perceptions in interviewers, and these traits may or may not be related to the job.[64] Of all the recommendations for adding structure, the best way to ensure that interviewers treat each candidate fairly and to improve the chances of making good hiring decisions is to build a standard scoring key for each interviewer to use during the interview process.

Components of a Structured Interview Scoring Key

An effective scoring key is essential to ensuring that you score candidates' responses consistently, especially since you will often have multiple interviewers interviewing multiple candidates throughout the selection process. There are four components that every score key should include for an interview, and these apply to both phone and face-to-face interviews:

- *Interview question(s):* Each question should include some short background information to provide context and could consist of multiple questions (e.g., "What did you do yourself and what did you rely on others to do? What were the final results? Would you do anything differently?").
- *Question probes:* Often you will find that candidates can get offtrack while answering a question or simply are not answering the question with enough detail for you to accurately score them. In these cases, follow-up probes might be needed (e.g., "Can you just put me in the room and describe what happened as events unfolded?"). It's important that interviewers use the same set of probes for each candidate, so including those probes on the interview scoring sheet is crucial.
- *Note-taking:* It is important for the interviewers to take detailed notes. Provide a large space for this on your score sheet. We encourage organizations to structure their interview notes section according to three key elements of the response: situation, behavior, outcome (SBO).
- *Rating scale:* We suggest using behavioral anchored rating scales for each interview question. You would take the same approach to create these as you would for the work samples/simulations discussed in chapter 5.

See figure 6.1 for a sample structured interview question and notes page using the SBO model.

Figure 6.1

Sample question and notes page structured interviews

Question 4	Probes
Describe a situation where you gathered and analyzed data to make a decision. What steps did you take? What did you conclude?	• How did you gather and analyze the data? • What did you learn from the data? • What did you do with the new knowledge?

Answer:

Situation

Behavior

Outcome

The SBO model is a technique for ensuring that interviewers capture the following important and behaviorally based information from the applicants in their notes:

- Situation: The applicants must describe a specific event or situation that come from a previous job, student teaching experience, or volunteer experience. This information is often contextual and provides a backdrop for their "story."
- Behavior: The applicants must describe specific actions they took in that situation focusing on their own behavior. This is the most critical information to capture and where notes should be the most detailed.
- Outcome: The applicants must describe the final results of the situation, and these results should clearly link to the applicant's behavior. This might include what happened, how an event ended, what was accomplished, or what the applicant learned.

We recommend placing the rating scale (see figure 6.2) on a separate page from the question and notes page. Interviewers should ask a question, take thorough notes, and then move on to the next question without scoring the responses. Scoring responses should not happen until the end of the interview, when the candidate is not present. At the completion of the interview, interviewers should review their notes thoroughly and rate their answers to each question. If the rating scale is included on the same sheet as the note-taking space, the temptation will be too great to focus on the scale and not to listen closely to the candidate's response or take thorough notes.

Figure 6.2

Sample rating scale for structured interview scoring

Based on your notes, *circle the rating* below that best fits the candidate's response.

1	2	3	4	5
Gathered data but sources were not varied or relevant. Examined pros and cons only after making the decision.		Gathered data from multiple relevant sources. Weighed pros and cons of a single option before making the decision.	Gathered data from only the most relevant sources. Weighed pros and cons of various options and considered multiple perspectives before making the decision. Specifically referenced best practices and considered methods used by other classes/districts while formulating solutions.	

SUMMARY

Structured interviews are much more predictive of performance than unstructured interviews. While there are pros and cons to both phone and face-to-face interviews, phone interviews can be cost-effective when school districts need to filter large numbers of applications and sort through them in a short period of time. Every structured interview requires an interview score sheet to be used consistently across all job applicants, and each score sheet should contain interview questions, question probes, a note-taking section, and a rating scale.

7

DESIGNING VALID TEACHER OBSERVATIONS

It's reasonable to assume that that one of the best ways to predict how a teacher will behave in a classroom is to observe a candidate teaching a class. Watching a candidate engage students offers the hiring committee insight into how the candidate applies teaching knowledge, skills, and abilities to the classroom setting. The teaching demonstration provides information about a candidate beyond that gleaned from other methods because it involves seeing whether or not the candidate can perform actual job tasks. Candidates might offer well-rehearsed responses to interview questions as to how they think they would approach instruction, but direct observation shows whether or not the candidate can and does act on these ideas.

As we discussed in earlier chapters, various selection methods provide indicators or samples of work performance.[1] Teaching observation constitutes a realistic sample of essential job tasks and, as such, is often considered a work sample. With this

selection method, hiring committee members use fewer inferences when predicting future teaching behavior. In contrast,
other selection methods, such as a knowledge test, tell us much
about the potential for the candidate to be effective, but they
don't show us if the candidate can translate the knowledge into
the right behaviors. The overall quality of the educational setting is influenced by the social relationships between students
and teachers, the curricular content that is covered, the teacher's pedagogical approaches, and the order and organization in
the classroom—teaching observation captures all of these primary aspects contributing to educational quality.[2]

Despite the potentially valuable information gathered from
teaching observation, it's used less frequently than interviews
and other selection methods in hiring teachers.[3] Principals in
one study rated demonstrations and videotaped teaching as low
in importance and as seldom used at their own schools.[4] They
cited difficulty in uploading videos during the application process and a lack of time for teaching observations as the primary
reasons, but they also indicated a belief that applicants can
provide videos that misrepresent their teaching. Their reluc-
tance is understandable. Large numbers of applicants for few
teaching positions do render the time spent watching a demonstration a barrier to hiring efficiency. Furthermore, a videotaped demonstration of teaching could be the result of multiple "takes" and perhaps isn't indicative of how a candidate
would actually perform in a classroom. In addition, work sample or job performance tests, such as a teaching observation,
measure what people are *able* to do rather than what they actually *will* do on the job.[5] It could be that even those performing
the work well during selection do not do as well on the job af-

ter they have been hired because of lower motivation, poor supervision, lack of supplies, or other factors.[6] Certainly, during the hiring process candidates are motivated to perform their best on a teaching observation because they are aware of being observed, but this tells us little about their typical worker performance.[7]

Given the high validity of work samples, however, teaching observation emerges as a strong predictor of performance, one that might justify the time spent in order to identify better candidates.[8] In particular, with the increased use of video technology that can streamline evaluation time for human resources staff, this may become a more frequent method used to assess what teachers are capable of in the classroom.

RICH DATA: THE GOOD AND THE BAD

The teaching observation is similar to the interview in its ability to capture rich data. Candidate characteristics and personal qualities are more apparent, unlike the information contained in such selection methods as applications, essays, grade point average, and knowledge test results. Hiring decision makers (e.g., principals) often attend not only to professional qualifications but also to personal qualities, such as enthusiasm and appearance, when making selection decisions.[9] However, if applicant qualities are not related to the tasks required for the job, then these rich sources of data could provide information that leads hiring committees to choose less-qualified candidates. Suppose that a candidate exhibits charisma and, during the teaching observation, entertains the students and captures their interest. However, let's also suppose that this charismatic teacher is unable to assemble and deliver a clear lesson plan that effectively teaches students new material. The hiring committee might be unduly influenced by the candidate's charisma and overlook her inability to perform other essential functions of the job. A less charismatic candidate might be much more effective in delivering high-quality learning opportunities to students but goes unnoticed because he is less entertaining.

Nonverbal cues affect interviewers' or raters' judgments of applicant qualifications, even after accounting for variance in objective information.[10] Articulation, voice intensity, and the use of pauses influence ratings of applicant quality even more than clothing or cleanliness, presumably because the latter physical characteristics can be altered easily and might be perceived by raters as less stable.[11] One study found that visual cues (e.g., smiling, gaze, attractiveness) and, more strongly, vocal cues (e.g., pitch, speech rate, pauses) correlate with job performance ratings for managers, possibly because they positively affect raters' perceptions of candidates.[12] The authors of this study indicated that these characteristics serve a purpose for managerial effectiveness; perhaps this also applies to teaching. For example, say that students in a math class develop a stronger connection with their teacher, who exhibits these characteristics; perhaps these students learn more because they pay greater attention to the teacher because they like him. In this example, the teaching candidate who exhibits these cues also is an effective teacher. However, even if this is the case, it's important to make sure that other criteria of effectiveness (e.g., meeting learning objectives) can be sustained. The hiring committee might recognize that nonverbal cues likely affect ratings, but teaching effectiveness includes more than only nonverbal cues. Raters who are unduly influenced by these nonverbal cues might miss other actions apparent in the demonstration that strongly predict effectiveness, such as how organized the teacher is in presenting material.

Many studies have identified characteristics of raters and ratees that affect rater judgments. A recent study from the medical arena provides some insight into the cognitive bases of how ratings are made of professionals engaging with clients. In this study, faculty at teaching hospitals observed and rated residents who were engaged with patient care.[13] Similarities exist between faculty observing medical residents and school district hiring committees rating teaching candidates. Both residents and teachers receive extensive training at universities for their jobs. They are expected to enter the job with requisite knowledge, skills, and abilities developed from classes and practica. Both jobs include professional work, and both involve a large degree of interaction with clients (patients, students). Also, in the study, faculty rated residents on their interactions with clients/patients; in teaching observations, hiring committee members rate candidates on how they interact with clients/students.

The researchers identified cognitive themes that affected ratings. First, raters used different frames of reference in judging others' behaviors: themselves (e.g., "This is what I would do"), others (e.g., "How would other teachers deal with this situation?"), or professional standards. Using different frames of reference for evaluating behavior influenced their observations and their ratings. Second, they inferred meaning during their observations from residents' actions (e.g., crossed arms), and these inferences differed across raters. Third, raters struggled with translating their judgments from their observations to numerical ratings; in many cases, they complained of limited guidelines or definitions for the ratings. Finally, the researchers identified contextual factors (e.g., ratee's past performance, relationship between rater and ratee) that influenced observations and subsequent ratings.

Research is lacking in identifying rater characteristics that influence whether or not individuals will be able to objectively evaluate teacher quality from observations, even if they are trained.[14] More effective raters need to understand content domain (e.g., effective teaching behavior).[15] It's unclear to what extent experience and training in education influence raters' observation skills; however, raters may exhibit bias in their ratings of the teaching demonstration if their beliefs differ from scoring standards or the values that are apparent in the observed classroom.[16] Raters who take an adult-centered approach to education differ in their ratings from those taking a child-centered approach. There are also differences in how raters value behaviors that are not reflected or are counter to those included in the way the teaching observation is scored.[17] These findings resonate with issues medical school faculty experienced in rating residents when they interjected their own ideas as a frame of reference (e.g., "I would do it differently").

These research findings suggest that, as much as we wish to rate candidates accurately, we have limitations in recording and assessing behavior. Unfortunately, our rating accuracy influences how accurately we can predict candidate performance; thus, validity suffers the more we let extraneous factors influence our ratings. Although we established in chapter 3 that it's impossible to have perfect validity, we can take steps to limit factors that undermine the validity of teaching demonstrations.

STRUCTURING TEACHING OBSERVATIONS

As with unstructured interviews, approaching an observation in an unstructured way will likely yield results that are inconsistent between raters and that have low validity in predicting future performance. We can imagine how easily different members of the hiring committee might emphasize unique perspectives of teaching that they deem important or allow various candidate characteristics to unduly influence them. Like other selection methods, however, structuring the observation increases our potential for evaluating candidates consistently and against job-relevant criteria.

In chapter 7 we discussed how interviews exist on a continuum from completely unstructured to highly structured and identified characteristics of structure from the employment literature.[18] We can apply some of those same characteristics to teaching observations. For example, we might improve a teaching demonstration by basing its requirements on the essential tasks identified in a job analysis. We're then asking candidates to demonstrate knowledge, skills, and abilities that will be used on the job, such as developing and following a lesson plan or developing examples and exercises for demonstrating complex ideas. As some researchers note, observing samples of current teachers' behavior in the classroom could be influenced by any number of factors, like student distractions about an upcoming sporting event; also, principals might choose a time to observe teachers when they are not engaging in behaviors that truly represent the quality of instruction.[19] To the extent that the observation doesn't capture the true potential of the candidate or does not provide information about job-relevant tasks, it will be a deficient selection method for predicting future performance.

Analogous to asking the same questions across candidates in an interview, candidates should be given specific requirements for videotaped demonstrations if those are to be used in the hiring process; this allows for consistent evaluation across candidates. Videotaped teaching demonstrations might be more convenient for hiring committees if there are limited opportunities for setting up an observation (e.g., class is not in session). However, interview research suggests that ratings of videotaped performance versus face-to-face performance differ. One study found that interviewers rated candidates in face-to-face interviews higher than when those same candidates were evaluated based on a videotaped interview.[20] In light of these findings, committees might consider the need for sticking with one format for all candidates.

As with interviews, a more consistent and potentially more valid evaluation of a teaching demonstration could be made if detailed rating scales are used. This aspect of standardization addresses one of the cognitive struggles mentioned earlier when medical school faculty attempted to rate residents' interactions with clients. In that study, faculty commented on the difficulty of translating their observations to rating scales due to little guidance.[21] Detailed rating scales reduce the complexity of translating responses or behaviors to a scoring system.

Additional practices to increase standardization include having raters take detailed notes, using multiple raters, using the same raters across demonstrations, and providing rater training. Recent concerns over teacher observation for gauging effectiveness address some of these issues. Principals often rate teaching observations individually; the lack of input from

144

other raters allows for single raters to use the observation in unintended ways, and it may reaffirm the idea that observation is being evaluated in an ad hoc manner.[22] Furthermore, to the extent that raters engage in idiosyncratic evaluation (e.g., one rater tends to be more lenient than the other), it is advantageous for selection decision making to include that rater (and her rating effect) across candidates for the job.

A challenge facing a hiring committee trying to evaluate a teaching demonstration is its free-form nature. With an interview, members of the hiring committee familiarize themselves with the questions and prompts before the interview begins. Once the interview starts, committee members control the pace of the interview through how quickly they question the candidate, the focus of the interview through the questions themselves, and the interactions during the interview (e.g., acknowledging responses, asking for clarification). However, observations, whether live or videotaped, are controlled less by the hiring committee and might vary more from candidate to candidate, especially if candidates are asked to teach to a group of students in an existing class. Thus, a structured teaching demonstration lacks some of the controls found in a structured interview. Although some researchers indicate that a highly structured interview minimizes the need for interviewer training, training needs continue to exist for raters evaluating teaching demonstrations, even for observations that are relatively structured.[23]

TRAINING RATERS

The literature on teaching observation has strongly called for the need to train raters.[24] Much of what we know about documenting observation comes from performance appraisal literature.

For years researchers have grappled with the difficulty of observing and evaluating worker behavior in a reliable and valid manner.

Various approaches to training raters have been used to decrease the potential for rating error and for increasing accuracy of ratings. Three approaches that apply to rating teaching demonstrations are performance dimension training, frame-of-reference (FOR) training, and behavioral observation training. Performance dimension training involves familiarizing raters with the dimensions to be used for evaluating behavior *before* the rater observes behavior. FOR training focuses on providing raters with common performance standards for evaluating behaviors. Behavioral observation training involves enhancing raters' skill in recording behavioral events (e.g., note taking).[25] Meta-analytic research has established that all three types of training increase rating accuracy, with FOR training resulting in the largest increase of rating accuracy.[26] This accuracy can be maintained even after a two-week delay between training and the time ratings are made.[27] Other research has found that FOR training improves the number of behaviors that raters can recall from observation, but by itself it does not improve the quality of the recall. Combining FOR training with behavior observation training improves the quality of the information that raters recall from their observations.[28] These findings suggest that school districts that use live or video-taped demonstrations as a selection method should incorporate rater training when preparing hiring committee members. School districts could potentially increase accuracy in assessments of teaching by determining performance standards or defining what effective performance involves and training hiring committee members to use these standards in rating performance. To accomplish this, one or more "ideal" teaching scenarios would be videotaped and referred to during rater training to illustrate optimal performance on each of the areas included in the evaluation form.

USING TEACHING OBSERVATION

Teaching observations often are used for assessing practicing teachers in order to document effectiveness, but they also can be useful for predicting teaching success if utilized as a selection method. In this chapter we have summarized research findings that suggest ways for making teaching observation a more viable and accurate selection method. Now let's work through an example that could be applied for hiring teachers for a school.

You've determined that "Instructional Delivery" is a critical skill that teachers must possess to be effective. (Hint: The appearance of this KSAO on your list of must-haves should not be shocking.) This is a skill that could be measured through a live teaching observation or a videotaped teaching demonstration. As an example, "Classroom Management" would not be well suited for a videotaped demonstration, since it would be difficult to assess the extent to which students were engaged in the lesson and to gauge the quality of the teacher/student interactions solely from a videotape. A skill like this should be measured in a live setting. But you can get a good sense of the teacher's instructional delivery with both a live and videotaped teaching sample. It's important to create a detailed rating scale (or checklist) that provides all of the behaviors the teacher should be performing when truly providing exemplary instructional delivery. Again, this is where you pull in your SMEs and determine what behaviors or criteria belong on that checklist. What behaviors or criteria separate a poor teacher from an average teacher, and which separate the average teacher from the superior teacher? For this example, let's say that you've identified the following seven behaviors/criteria as critical to a teacher's instructional delivery:

- Presents material clearly and accurately
- Makes sure material is an accurate reflection of the lesson plan
- Uses correct syntax, grammar, and spelling throughout the lesson
- Begins by clearly communicating lesson objective
- Checks for understanding and adjusts instructional delivery as needed
- Provides adequate time for students to respond
- Paces lesson and balances instructional time with student participation

You have determined that the first three of these behaviors are critical criteria; the teacher *must* perform these correctly to be effective. You will want to be certain that your raters pay extra attention to these three behaviors.

Next you create a rating/score sheet with these behaviors similar to that in figure 7.1. Note that the critical criteria are listed in bold type. It is also valuable to track separately how many critical criteria were met in addition to the regular behaviors. This way, if two candidates receive identical scores on the teaching observation, the candidate with a larger number of critical criteria met can be viewed more favorably. You also have to determine the pass/fail criteria, and this will largely depend on the

Figure 7.1

Sample score sheet for teaching observation/video

Applicant's name: _____

Evaluation criteria (please mark a check next to all criteria that are observed)	Criteria observed (total number of check marks)	Were all "critical criteria" (those listed in bold) observed? (Y/N)
Instructional Delivery		
• **Presents material clearly and accurately**		
• **Makes sure material is an accurate reflection of the lesson plan**		
• **Uses correct syntax, grammar, and spelling throughout the lesson**		
• Begins by clearly communicating lesson objective		
• Checks for understanding and adjusts instructional delivery as needed		
• Provides adequate time for students to respond		
• Paces lesson and balances instructional time with student participation		

Scoring summary for: _____

Category	Instructional delivery	Interpersonal relationships	Classroom management	Total
Met critical criteria? (Y/N)				
Applicant's score (number of observed criteria)				
Score necessary to proceed	5			
				Pass Fail

149

number of teachers you need to screen out. Here it's set at about 70 percent (the candidate must meet 70 percent of the behaviors to pass). If set at 90 percent or even 100 percent, it would obviously screen out a much larger number of applicants.

SUMMARY

Detailed rating scales help reduce the complexity of translating applicant behaviors or responses to a scoring system. In addition to a detailed rating scale, other practices to increase standardization include having raters take detailed notes, using multiple raters, using the same raters across demonstrations, and providing rater training. School districts could potentially increase accuracy in assessments of teaching by determining performance standards or defining what effective performance involves and training hiring committee members to use these standards in rating performance. Research suggests that school districts using live or videotaped demonstrations as a selection method should incorporate rater training when preparing hiring committee members.

8

COMBINING RESULTS TO MAKE FINAL HIRING DECISIONS

Think about the last time you made a substantial decision, such as buying a car. What information did you consider? Were there some features that you simply could not do without, such as an automatic transmission? Perhaps you walked in wanting a red car, but the salesperson pointed out that the silver car had an entertainment package that you liked; would you decide that the entertainment system was important enough to override your color preference? Even the decision to buy a car requires that you consider a wide range of data: repair history, price, fuel consumption, horsepower, acceleration rate, safety features, seating space, storage, and more. In order to make this decision, you distinguish in advance of arriving at the car dealership the "must-have" from the "nice-to-have" features and determine which criteria the car must meet before a decision can be made. The way that we process information about buying a car is not unlike the method we might use for selecting an employee, although employee selection is arguably much more complex.

Suppose a school district is hiring for four teaching positions and 100 candidates apply for these jobs. Each applicant submits an application, completes one work sample, participates in a structured interview, and provides a videotaped demonstration of teaching. With four selection methods for each of the 100 applicants, the selection committee must consider at least 400 pieces of information to make four hires. Not only is this task cognitively complex, but it is also time consuming and expensive. Assuming that the school district needs to have the four new teachers on the job as soon as possible, this screening method is not very practical.

In this scenario, each of the selection methods is considered equal in terms of importance and quality; all candidates provide data for all instruments. However, we know that some selection methods will provide us with more accurate predictions of teaching performance. We can assume, though, that few hiring committee members would be able to keep this much information organized in their minds; anyone who has participated on one of these committees realizes that candidates' responses tend to run together after even just the first few interviews. In order to keep the data straight and ensure that candidates are judged fairly on the basis of their responses, districts need standardized tools for comparing responses.

Without standardized tools that dictate the weight and position of each data point, responses from less valid methods (e.g., references) might unintentionally carry more weight than responses from more valid methods (e.g., a structured interview). Without a structure for comparing candidate responses, hiring team biases and preexisting assumptions sneak into the confused mass of data to erode the validity of each selection tool. We should be using research-based selection methods to simplify the task of choosing a successful candidate, not complicate it. But without a framework in place for systematically comparing applicants, we could end up choosing those who stand out for some reason (most attractive, most extroverted, most recently interviewed, funniest stories, etc.) and overlook those who excel on the job-related KSAOs our hiring tools are intended to measure. In short, we need a game plan for how to organize the data from our valid hiring tools in order to facilitate effective decision making when comparing candidates.

SEQUENCING OF SELECTION TOOLS

One of the first design features to consider when building a selection system is the order in which each selection tool is presented. Does the live interview come first or the teaching observation? When we look at the selection methods from the example—application, work sample, structured interview, and teaching observation—each method tells us something different about the applicant. For example, the application form helps us determine which applicants meet the minimum educational requirements for the job and allows us to compare candidates on their work experience and references. This doesn't mean that we will be able to choose the most qualified person for the job based only on the application form. But the application form does help us identify applicants who simply can't be considered for the job because they do not have the minimum qualifications or because they have negative references. Thus, the application form serves as an excellent choice to be the first step in narrowing the applicant pool.

153

Again, it is helpful to think of narrowing your applicant pool as using a funnel. The top of the funnel is broad and can accommodate greater mass, just as a job posting attracts applications from a large pool of potential employees. The application form helps identify unqualified applicants, who are then rejected or selected out of the process, much like the narrowing of the funnel. The applicants who remain meet the minimum qualifications of the job and could, in theory, perform the essential functions of the job.

Yield Ratio

At each stage of the hiring process when a selection method is used, additional candidates will be rejected, and some will choose to remove themselves from further consideration. It could be that these candidates wish to pursue opportunities elsewhere, have received job offers, or have decided that they aren't a good fit with the current position or the hiring school. As a result, fewer and fewer candidates proceed to the final stage of the selection process. Over time, districts can track the statistics of how many candidates stay in the process at each step compared to how many initially applied. These statistics will be valuable in helping refine hiring tools and plan future searches.

In the earlier example, suppose that of the four positions open, we fill only one; out of 100 applicants, only one qualified candidate was found. We review statistics from the last five years and find similar ratios between hiring and applicants. It could be that the applicants were not highly qualified, so fewer were hired, or that the applicants accepted jobs at other schools. Whatever the reason, we discover that we need approximately 100 applicants to fill one job. This is our yield ratio. So when our spring hiring begins, and we determine that we need to fill four positions, we know that our applicant pool should consist of at least 400 applicants (400:4) given our past yield ratio of 100:1.

Pass Rate/Selection Ratio

A related concept to the yield ratio is the pass rate or selection ratio. This statistic is calculated by dividing the number of people hired by the number of applicants for the job. A pass rate can be computed for each selection tool, and, depending on a range of elements such as the recruiting pool base rate and the difficulty of each selection tool, the pass rate may vary from tool to tool and even from year to year. One complication with the selection ratio is that organizations may define "applicant" differently based on their own recruitment and selection procedures.[1] As a result, some organizations consider only qualified applicants in their selection ratios, instead of all applicants, which is the case with the yield ratio. We use this more restrictive definition here as an example, but keep in mind that the selection ratio can be calculated the same way the yield ratio was calculated.

The selection ratio can be expressed as a percentage. For example, suppose you hire one person from 100 applicants. Your yield ratio is .01, or 1 percent. However, suppose that of the 100 applicants, only twenty meet the minimum educational requirements for the job. Your selection ratio is one person hired for the job divided by twenty candidates (1/20), which is .05, or 5 percent. The selection ratio indicates how selective the organization is or can be in hiring candidates. A low selection ratio (near 0) indicates that fewer qualified applicants are hired from among those who apply; either few were hired and/or many applied. And a high selection ratio (near 1.0 or 100 percent) indicates that most or all of the candidates who applied are hired, with a selection ratio of 100 percent indicating that every applicant meeting minimum qualifications is hired. In the example, if you have four positions and hire the only four qualified candidates, you would have a selection ratio of 100 percent. Perhaps all of these candidates were exceptional, but it's more likely that the high selection ratio means that you hired anyone meeting minimum qualifications who would be acceptable for the positions.

Relationship Among Yield Ratios, Selection Ratios, and Validity

We can calculate and review yield ratios and selection ratios at each step in the hiring process by calculating the number of applicants (for yield ratios) or qualified applicants (for selection ratios) that pass the selection method. Selection methods with higher selection ratios mean that the organization is less selective and is likely hiring a mix of top performers as well as adequate performers. Those with lower selection ratios pass fewer candidates, and, presumably, those who do pass represent the best of the candidate pool.

Although the selection ratio indicates how selective the organization can be when making decisions, it only reflects the numbers of candidates passing the selection methods, not whether those passing truly are better performers or are better hires in some way. It could be that these selection methods, if not valid, are screening candidates out, but they are screening out the most effective candidates and passing the average candidates. This is why validity is an important consideration when comparing candidates and examining the selection funnel. A selection method that shows higher validity means that the selection method is more accurate in its predictions of some outcomes (such as job performance) than one that shows lower validity. A higher validity means making fewer errors in selection based on using the selection method. That is, when using a highly valid selection tool, you're more likely to reject candidates who would have performed poorly on the job and more likely to pass candidates who will be successful on the job. A validity near .00 on a selection method means that people who score poorly on the test are no more likely to underperform on the job than people with high scores on the test; scores on the assessments will not predict performance. A validity near 1.0 means that you can predict an outcome with certainty; high scorers on the selection test will be high performers on the job, and those with low scores will perform poorly on the job.

A school district that uses a work sample with a validity coefficient with performance of .50 will more accurately predict future performance of its candidates than the district that uses an unstructured interview with a validity of .11. The district using the unstructured interview with the lower validity will be more likely to make selection mistakes than will the district using the work sample with the higher validity; these mistakes could result in hiring those who pass the test and turn out to be poor performers (false positives) or not hiring those who fail the test and would have been excellent performers (false negatives). Of the two, the false negatives are opportunity costs, and, although the school district could have benefited from hiring these individuals, its more significant problems are the teachers it hired who are not performing well (false positives). Compare figure 8.1, which demonstrates a selection tool with a low validity (it's correlation to job performance is low), to figure 8.2, which demonstrates a selection tool with high validity (it's correlation to job performance is relatively strong):

Figure 8.1

Selection tool with low validity

- The high validity tool has many more good hires (true positives) than the low validity tool
- The high validity tool has far fewer bad hires (false positives) than the low validity tool
- The low validity tool has many more missed opportunities (false negatives) than the high validity tool
- The low validity tool has far fewer mistakes avoided (true negatives) than the high validity tool

Base Rate of Success

While it might be appealing to think that whittling a candidate pool down to a few people using valid selection measures en-

Figure 8.2
Selection tool with high validity

sures success in hiring, there is an additional issue to consider: the base rate of success that exists in the recruiting pool. If you hired all those who applied for the job without using your selection methods, what percentage would be successful? This percentage refers to the recruiting pool base rate of success.[2] While you will never know the precise recruiting pool base rate, considering the relative strength of the recruiting pool can significantly affect the way you structure your hiring process. If all applicants are successful (a recruiting pool base rate of 100 percent), then your selection methods add no value; nothing could improve your 100 percent chance of success in hiring. If your base rate is 0, meaning that no applicants would be successful, then it's unlikely that your selection methods will help. A base rate of 50 percent suggests that half of your applicants would be successful on the job anyway, so in this case your valid selection methods will help identify which of these candidates to hire (hopefully, with the assistance of valid selection methods, you identify the 50 percent who will be successful).

To illustrate the concepts we've just discussed, let's return to our example. Of our 100 applicants for our four teaching positions, we expect that about 50 would be successful. This is our base rate of success. This means that valid selection methods can be useful in helping us pick out these 50 people. When we check their applications, only 90 meet minimum qualifications. We then use three selection methods with reasonably high validities—work sample, structured interview, and teaching observation—to narrow our pool to 10 candidates. Of those 10, we offer jobs to 5, and 3 accept. Our yield ratio is 100:3, or 3 percent. Our selection ratio, if we define applicants as only the people who meet minimum qualifications, is .0333, or 3.33 percent (3/90). This means that we are selective. Based on the high validities of our selection methods, we feel fairly confident that we are accurately identifying the candidates who are likely to perform well. We have the best situation for selecting high-quality applicants.

MULTIPLE CUTOFF VERSUS COMPENSATORY METHODS

What order of selection methods is most effective in identifying the best candidates? Should we assess each candidate on all selection methods and combine each person's scores, or should we set up the selection methods so that candidates are only considered for job offers if they pass each selection method? Both approaches have their strengths. The first approach, in which candidates are only considered if they meet minimum scores on all selection methods, is the multiple cutoff model (sometimes referred to as the multiple hurdles approach). The second approach, in which all scores are combined, is the compensatory approach, because it allows a higher score on one selection method to compensate for a lower score on another selection method.

Multiple Cutoff Approach

When using a multiple cutoff approach, pass/fail scores are set for each selection method. This can be done a number of ways, but generally the cutoff score should relate to the level of proficiency needed for critical KSAOs of the job, and they should be high enough to make sure that minimum job performance standards are met.[3] For example, if a job requires that workers are able to lift 150 pounds, the passing score for the strength portion of the physical ability test would be set at 150 pounds. Continuing with the sample situation, our 100 applicants for the teaching position would be asked to complete an application and then participate in all selection methods. Once these were completed, we would score each person's performance and eliminate those failing one or more selection assessments. Those we consider for job offers would be the applicants who passed all assessments; their performance met or exceeded the minimum passing requirements set for each selection method.

The minimum cutoff method is particularly useful if new hires must meet a minimum requirement of proficiency or ability that cannot be compensated for or substituted with another attribute. For example, firefighters must be able to use their physical ability to operate equipment and pull or carry victims to safety. A firefighter with a conscientious personality and knowledge of firefighting principles might be successful in some parts of the job, but if the firefighter isn't physically able to lift or drag a person to safety or operate equipment, she cannot perform some essential functions of the job. No other quality can compensate for that physical ability. Similarly, teachers must possess the education and credentials to teach; experience and enthusiasm alone can't compensate for not having the minimum required education and credentials. Therefore, applicants must meet these requirements in order to be considered for the job.

It is important to ask yourself two questions when identifying the KSAOs that are required for teachers to perform the various functions of their job:

- Which KSAOs are absolutely critical for them to successfully perform the job?
- Of the critical KSAOs, must the teachers possess them on hire or can they be reasonably trained on the job?

One concern with using a minimum cutoff approach is that all applicants are evaluated using each selection method. If many applicants express interest in a teaching job, hiring committees might find themselves spending countless hours interviewing and observing those who do not meet minimum requirements in other areas, such as education or references. One variant of this multiple cutoff approach is to view the selection methods as hurdles. Much like track runners who must clear hurdles, candidates in a multiple hurdle system must pass one hurdle (selection method) to remain a contender and move on to the next selection assessment.

We know that it will take far too much time to evaluate all 100 of our applicants for our four teaching positions. Trying to coordinate the calendars of hiring committee members and each interviewee poses problems during our tight spring hiring timeframe. If our recruiting pool base rate is approximately 50 percent, then about half of these applicants would not be successful on the job. The application form requires that applicants list their education, experience, credentialing, and references, and respond to a few problem-solving questions. We decide to set the application form as our first hurdle to ensure that applicants meet the minimum requirements in these areas based on the job description. Ten of the 100 applicants do not meet these requirements; we screen out 10 percent of the pool at this hurdle before moving to the next. Again, we see the funnel effect. The next hurdle we set is a brief, structured phone interview, requiring all candidates to speak with a trained interviewer from our selection committee over the phone in a thirty-minute, seven-question interview. Each candidate's phone interview is scored using a scoring key with BARs for each rating scale. We can use either a predetermined pass/fail point or simply rank order the candidates based on their scores and pass those with the highest scores. The passing candidates then move to the next selection assessment. See figure 8.3 for a sample score sheet for a multiple cutoffs (hurdles) approach. (In this example, the candidate passed the first hurdle but not the second, so the final decision was not to hire.)

Although this multiple cutoffs approach reduces the candidate pool and protects the organization from spending resources on candidates who do not meet important requirements, it takes time to move from one assessment to the next. Depending on the selection methods used, some organizations

Figure 8.3
Sample score sheet for multiple cutoffs (hurdles) model

Teacher selection overall score sheet

Candidate name: *Connie Mack*

Evaluator name	Date	Score (1 to 100)	Decision (Pass-conditional-fail)
Phase 1: Phone screen	3/17/14	88	Pass
Phase 2: Job sample	4/1/14	38	Fail
Phase 3: Principal interview	None	N/A	N/A

Notes:			
This candidate should not be eligible for future applications. Based on observations during the teaching sample, his Phase I answers contained blatantly misleading information about prior teaching experience.	Final decision:		Don't hire
	Final evaluator signature:	Jane Sample	
	Date:	4/7/14	

might test all applicants using multiple selection methods in one day. With interviews and other time-consuming methods typically used to hire teachers, a multiple hurdles approach generally proves more efficient, especially given the pressure to make rapid decisions during a spring hiring push.

Compensatory Approach

In some cases, it isn't necessary for candidates to meet minimum criteria in all areas; instead, it's possible, and even likely, that candidates can make up for deficits in one area with strong performance in another, or that candidates can be trained in deficient areas on the job. Consider a sales position in which applicants are evaluated on their communication skills as part of the interview process. They are later evaluated in a simulated sales call role-play. Candidates might be nervous during the interview and fail to exhibit effective communication skills; however, during the role-play, these same candidates create shared understanding with clients and smoothly address their concerns. Combining interview scores with role-play scores would allow one strong score to compensate for a weaker score. The compensatory model calls for combining scores on two or more selection methods to form an overall assessment score.

COMBINING SCORES

If a selection process consists of only one selection method, such as a structured interview, the overall score equals that of the one method. It's fairly straightforward to identify which candidates scored better on the interview and to proceed with making job offers. However, most selection systems contain more than one selection method, and many use a compensatory approach to combine separate assessment scores into one overall score. This can pose problems if the selection methods use different scales of measurement.

Suppose we use a rubric to evaluate teaching portfolios, with the lowest score a 1 and the highest score a 10. We use a structured interview that is based on a 100-point scale. And, finally, we score teaching observation from 1 to 50. We would like to create an overall assessment score for our candidates based on the scores from these three separate selection methods, but if we simply sum the scores, we would be giving less weight to the teaching portfolio and the greatest weight to the structured interview. Since we want them all to count the same, we need to

165

convert the scores to a consistent metric. We can standardize the scores, such as using z-scores, or we could convert all the scores to one scale of measurement. For example, we could easily do this by multiplying the portfolio score by 10 to make it a 100-point scale and multiplying the observation score by 2 to convert it to a 100-point scale. Once we have all scores on the same scale of measurement, we can sum them to obtain an overall assessment score. For example, a candidate scoring a 90 on the interview, a 45 on the teaching observation, and an 8 on the portfolio, would earn an overall score of $((8 * 10) + 90 + (45 * 2)) = 80 + 90 + 90 = 260$. Figure 8.4 provides a sample score sheet for this specific example of a compensatory approach that requires standardizing and combining scores.

In some instances, we might decide that one selection method score should carry more weight than others. For example, our structured interview and teaching observation may have higher validity for predicting performance than the teaching portfolio does (as determined through validation research discussed in section 3 of chapter 9). As a result, we decide to weight those two assessments more in the overall score. Once we convert the individual scores to a standard scale, we can then weight the scores and sum them to arrive at an overall assessment score. We determine that the interview should be weighted at 40 percent, the teaching observation at 40 percent, and the portfolio at 20 percent. Our new assessment score based on our earlier example would be $((80 * .20) + (90 * .40) + (90 * .40)) = (16 + 36 + 36) = 88$.

It is important to note that the decisions about weighing each component of the hiring system should not be done randomly. Instead, this should be done using a systematic method typically involving a careful analysis of subject matter opinions

Figure 8.4

Sample score sheet for compensatory model

Teacher selection overall score sheet

Candidate name: *Branch Rickey*

	Phase 1 Interview	Phase 2 Teacher observation	Phase 3 Portfolio	
Raw score	90	45	8	
Score adjustment	No adjustment	Score above x 2	Score above x 10	Total score:
Total	90	90	80	260

Notes:			
	Final decision:	Hire	Don't hire
	Final evaluator signature:		
	Date:		

along with specific research on the effects of various weighting options on validity. We might present a group of five SMEs with a handful of options about how to weight each assessment and then assess the extent to which those SMEs agree on the weights. We would not settle on the final weighting until we had at least three or perhaps even four of the five agreeing on the final weighting scheme. In assessing these judgments, we would need to be sure each SME was providing independent judgments so they are not influencing each other's views. Without clear and compelling evidence about the strength of weights that can be applied to each assessment, the best approach is to weight them all equally.

COMPARING CANDIDATES

Once the assessment scores have been computed for each candidate, or the last hurdle has been cleared, it's time to identify which candidates should be offered jobs. There are a number of ways to compare candidates using their scores. The first is to rank order the candidates from highest score to lowest score and then offer jobs to the top scorers. This method is simple and easy to administer, and no cutoff score is needed.[4] However, once the candidates are ranked, the rank order does not indicate how far apart the candidates are in their scores. The candidate ranked number two on the list could have performed much lower than did the top candidate, and candidate three could have been just slightly lower than candidate two in overall score. Ranking also does not indicate how well the candidates have performed against a standard; that is, the top ranked candidate could have performed much lower than the organization would expect a candidate to perform.

Another method for making decisions is to choose a cut score for the overall assessment. Candidates scoring at or above the cut score pass, and those scoring below it fail. The cut score can be readjusted over time to allow the organization to choose only the highest performers on the assessments (raising the cut score) or to choose more candidates to meet the needs of the organization (lowering the cut score).

Recalling the earlier discussion of false negatives and false positives, false positives are those who pass the assessment cutoff but are ultimately unsuccessful on the job. Raising the cut score reduces the number of false positives; with the new, higher cut score, most likely those who pass will actually perform well on the job given a strong enough validity for the selection methods. However, by raising the cut score, more candidates fail who probably would have been successful on the job, thus increasing the number of false negatives. This might be a good approach when the risk of a hiring mistake is great, such as selecting nurses, who make decisions that impact the health and safety of hospital patients.

Lowering the cutoff score decreases the number of false negatives; individuals who would be successful on the job but scored lower on the assessment now pass the assessment. However, lowering the cut score also increases the number of false positives. For school districts, choosing a low performer might affect student achievement, funding, and other important outcomes. Also, lowering the cut score means hiring more and more of the candidate pool, thereby reducing selectivity and increasing the selection ratio. It doesn't really help to have selection methods that predict performance when hiring the good and the bad performers.

Another method for determining which candidates to hire is banding. However, the banding approach accounts for the lack of reliability in candidates' scores. It's rare to have perfect reliability of measurement, especially when assessing people. The width of bands is generally established based on the standard error of measurement.[5] The candidates falling within each band are considered as having the same score, although their scores might differ from each other slightly. For example, candidates Bob, Gina, and Clyde scored 38, 36, and 34, respectively. Based on the less-than-perfect reliability in scoring, we determine that they fall within the same band. Brad, Jenny, and Cindy scored 31, 30, and 27, respectively. They fall into the second band, and their scores are considered the same. When offering jobs, we could choose any one of the candidates from the first band (Bob, Gina, or Clyde) without having to choose Bob first. Perhaps Bob did not fit as well with the other teachers; we could choose Gina or Clyde instead.

SUMMARY

We present in this chapter options for a teacher hiring process that is designed primarily for the big push of hiring that happens in many districts every spring. However, the selection process and the decisions that are made about scoring should be adaptable for ongoing hiring when unexpected vacancies emerge. The comparing of applicants is a very complex aspect of the selection process. In the ideal scenario, you have a large number of candidates and therefore can be selective. Valid selection tools help most when your selection ratio is low (you are *not* hiring most of your applicant pool). There are pros and cons to each of the various approaches to running candidates through the selection process. You have to determine which makes the most sense for your organization.

9

MAXIMIZING YOUR
HIRING BUDGET

Ideally, school districts would dedicate effort and financial
resources to improving their selection systems and make
data-driven decisions about candidates. Realistically, though,
districts often face scarce resources and must phase in improvements. Despite the constraints, they can adjust their practices
to have a positive effect on hiring. In this chapter we introduce
three levels of effort/expense that can be implemented by a district to improve student results through hiring better teachers.
In the first section we suggest how districts can improve selection results by making changes to their current processes. The
second section outlines how to identify untapped competency
areas to assess with new selection tools while considering important outcomes such as applicant reactions. And the third
section describes how the use of large-scale validation studies
can identify which selection methods are working and should
be retained, as well as which ones are not working and should

be discarded. In this final section we also discuss how validation data can be used to order the selection methods in the hiring process so that school districts can better use their limited resources.

I. SMALL ADJUSTMENTS FOR BIG RESULTS

Many districts have very little dedicated staff time to build all new hiring tools. However, districts can make significant improvements to their existing tools with a minimal amount of time and effort.

Suppose a district is using several job-related interview questions but has no standard method for asking the questions; they are asked in different order each time and are often paraphrased. Nor does it have any consistent method for recording and scoring candidate responses; instead, interviewers rely on their intuition to identify the candidate with the best overall responses to the questions. The questions capture job-related information and have the potential for serving as strong predictors of job performance, so the framework exists for effectively selecting the right candidate for the job. However, in its current state, the interview most likely does not live up to its potential as a strong predictor of performance: it isn't conducted in the same manner each time, no scoring key exists so that interviewers can score consistently, and there's no one method for comparing candidates. Intuition informs the decision-making process. As a result, the district can't readily determine how candidates truly differ from each other in their interview performances. Substantial improvements can be made to this interview, however, if the district makes progress toward standardization.

Standardizing existing tools represents a lower-cost, lower-effort option for districts. They could reformat existing tools (or most of them) so that they are more standardized and develop scoring protocols to use consistently across all applicants (some of the samples used in this book could serve as templates). In particular, districts can gain significant improvements in their existing selection systems by starting with three things:

1. Standardize the process for all applicants
2. Standardize scoring across observers
3. Create a scoring grid to record scores and compare applicants

Objectivity and Subjectivity

Each selection method provides us with information that we can use to make decisions about candidates. Much of the data we collect during selection is based on our judgment. Motivation, for example, has no physical properties; we can't measure it using a scale or a ruler. Rather, applicant motivation must be inferred from information the applicant provides; those inferences we make require judgment. Suppose, for example, that a school district uses years of teaching experience, a teaching observation, and an interview to identify which candidates will receive job offers. How much judgment goes into each of these measures? Objective measures are nonjudgmental, while subjective measures require judgment; objective measures are "direct measures of countable behaviors or outcomes," while subjective measures generally consist of ratings of a person's performance.[1] In this example, experience does not require the hiring committee to make a judgment; the hiring committee counts the number of years each candidate worked as a teacher. Thus, this measure is objective. However, the committee members judge responses to interview questions when making their ratings, and they judge the suitability of the candidates' approaches in the teaching sample when they observe it, whether in a video or in person. The selection methods themselves aren't necessarily objective or subjective; rather, objectivity and subjectivity refer to how we evaluate the information gleaned from using each method. For example, the teaching observation might require committee members to evaluate how effectively the teacher engaged students in a discussion; this requires judgment. However, tracking the total number of minutes the candidate spent on various activities during the teaching sample is an example of objective measurement.

At first glance, we might think of subjectivity or the use of judgment as bad or as hindering our efforts to uncover the best candidate from the pool of those who applied. After all, we often pride ourselves on being objective when making decisions. For example, you're considering where you would like to vacation next year. You narrow your choices to three. You read promotional literature, speak with friends who vacationed there in the past, and examine average temperatures for the week you plan to travel. The temperatures represent objective data, but the promotional literature and friends' accounts of their vacations represent subjective data. Let's say that in your assessment of the three vacation options, you collect the same types of data, evaluate those data against the same criteria (e.g., cost, ease of traveling to the location, passport requirements), and then make a decision. You have standardized your approach, but most of the data you considered involved making judgments and did not represent a truly objective measure. Thus, the colloquial use of *objective* clouds the distinction between data that is based on judgment and that based on nonjudgmental methods. We can be open-minded and rational when judging data in order to make decisions. Thus, our idea of being objective in selection can refer to measures that do not require our judgment (e.g., counting an applicant's years of experience) or to the extent we incorporate standardization into our evaluation of subjective data.

Judgment is a legitimate element of selecting candidates and, in fact, might be more helpful for effective decision making than relying solely on objective data. Not all aspects of performance can be measured objectively; "some key measures are necessarily subjective."[2] Relying only on objective measures overemphasizes those nonjudgmental aspects of candidate assessment (e.g., years of experience) at the expense of considering the job components that, for evaluation, require judgment (e.g., motivating students). Objective data, while less subject to rater bias, represent an "excessively narrow" view of performance.[3]

Meta-analytic research of performance appraisal data supports the contention that objective measures and subjective measures of the same constructs differ and should not be substituted for each other or used interchangeably; the measures capture different aspects of the criterion. For example, years of teaching experience (an objective measure) tells us something different about a teacher's likelihood of success than does an interview question asking candidates how they handled disruptive students in the past (a subjective measure). Both relate to past teaching performance, but each focuses on a unique aspect of performance. A teacher with two years' experience might have had a teaching assignment in a school fraught with student conduct issues, while another candidate with the same years of experience had no encounters with disruptive behavior. Thus, there is a place for both objective and subjective measures of candidate performance. As researchers caution, "It is better to imperfectly measure relevant dimensions than to perfectly measure irrelevant ones."[4]

As we discussed in chapter 3, we cannot expect to reach a point of perfectly measuring constructs like knowledge or motivation. Measures of performance, whether objective or subjective, may not fully capture what we're intending to measure. Suppose we want to measure candidates' knowledge of their teaching field. We count the classes they took in the field, examine their grade point averages, and rate their teaching demonstrations on the basis of how well they explained the subject matter. Despite the use of these objective and subjective measures, however, we probably didn't capture the full level of knowledge each candidate possesses; instead, we sampled their knowledge. Our measures are somewhat deficient in measuring subject knowledge because they don't measure every aspect of subject knowledge.

Likewise, measures could be influenced by factors unrelated to our criterion (e.g., subject matter knowledge). For example, a candidate's grade point average could reflect the college instructors' severe grading or lenient grading; some candidates have higher grade point averages not because they know their subject better but because they were enrolled in an easier program or had the fortune of taking classes from professors who were more lenient. Our ratings of the teaching demonstration could have been influenced by previous candidates' performance or the candidate's attractiveness or because the candidate reminds us of another teacher who is popular at our school or any other irrelevant factors. This is called *criterion contamination.* Generally, subjective measures are considered more susceptible to "contamination," and in some cases ratings may be affected by cognitive limitations that the raters have in processing information.[5] But we can easily take steps to minimize these sources of error. We accomplish this through standardization.

Standardization

Standardization is used to control extraneous factors that affect scores or ratings. This makes it more likely that the score or rating represents the attribute we intend to measure instead of an unrelated factor. A selection method does not have perfect prediction, but decreasing the effects of extraneous factors in measurement will help attain the best validity possible for that selection method. Standardization is an easy first step for districts to take for improving their selection systems; it requires little effort and can profoundly affect decision quality.

Suppose that a school district uses an interview to measure subject matter knowledge, motivation, and communication skills. The district establishes that these criteria or attributes are important to the job of teacher and that the interview is an appropriate method to use for measuring them. So far, so good. The hiring committee decides an unstructured interview would offer flexibility in assessing these characteristics, and each hiring committee member asks any number of questions of an applicant based on the applicant's initial response. As a result, each applicant fields different interview questions. Although this approach keeps applicants from sharing information with each other about the selection process, the content of the interview is not identical for all applicants. How can we be sure that the different questions we ask relating to subject matter knowledge are equally effective in tapping knowledge? It could be that a committee member poses a question to one applicant, "What motivates you to teach," while asking another, "How will you deal with low student motivation?" Both questions relate to motivation, but they are clearly different in their foci. It would be difficult, or even impossible, to compare responses across candidates based on these very different questions. Similarly, a question asking a candidate to explain how she dealt with her own low motivation in the past might generate a very different response than asking her how she would approach certain motivational challenges faced by many teachers in the district, such as a lack of parental support or low student achievement. Thus, an initial step in standardization is to ensure that the content of each selection method is identical for all applicants. In our example, all applicants should receive the opportunity to answer the same questions.

Test Integrity/Security.   One concern that you might have at this point is how you will protect the integrity of your selection system if each applicant receives the same questions. Wouldn't these questions be shared with other applicants over time? This is a realistic concern, but safeguards exist.

First, testing standards call for protecting the integrity of a test by keeping it in a secure location.[6] The hiring committee also can make sure that no questions or documents are given to applicants that identify the interview questions. Additionally, the district can develop multiple questions to measure an attribute but pretest them to establish that they are equivalent in content, response, and statistical characteristics.[7]

This last step will require some statistical work and additional effort and expense; generally, the classic approach to alternate test forms includes developing item pools, pretesting items to gather statistics about those items, and constructing the test so that it has certain constraints, such as having the items matched on difficulty and how well they discriminate based on levels of performance.[8] New items can be pretested with either applicants or current teachers. Teachers, for example, can be asked to volunteer as pseudo-applicants, with interviewers posing them multiple questions designed to measure the same attribute. The ratings or assessments on these questions can then be compared for each "candidate" and the reliability of the responses on the items documented. Questions of substantially similar difficulty with the same outcomes can be considered interchangeable for the interview. A similar approach could be used in testing new questions with applicants; the questions could be asked, compared to the existing questions, and not used in the final decision about candidate hiring. This approach capitalizes on applicants with high motivation, so they presumably will do their best in responding to the questions, but there is some concern that the applicants will remember these items and share them with others who apply for the job. In addition, an applicant who is rejected and reapplies in the future carries a potentially unfair advantage of having been exposed to the items earlier.[9] Clearly, districts need to make decisions about item content so that the integrity of the assessments is not compromised over time.

Standardizing Administration. This interview example represents a relatively straightforward approach to standardizing the selection instrument. However, assume that we also use a videotaped teaching demonstration as a selection method. When applicants submit an online application, we instruct them to upload a teaching demonstration. Unlike the interview, the hiring committee no longer retains control of content. We find that applicants vary in the content they include in their demonstration; some provide footage of their teaching in a classroom environment with students and demonstrate how they present material and respond to student questions. Others record themselves in a makeshift studio with no students present. They emphasize the subject matter, but they offer no insight into how they interact with students or answer questions. Consider the extraneous factors that potentially influence the ratings of these demonstrations: presence or absence of students; "real time" videotaping, complete with mistakes, versus a dubbed presentation with edits; the inclusion of extra features, such as responding to disruptive behavior. Myriad differences exist in the content of this assessment. Therefore, like an interview with different questions posed to each applicant, the demonstration lacks standardization. We cannot approach the demonstration in the same manner that we earlier suggested for the interview because the method is not one that is interactive; the hiring committee sees only the completed teaching demonstration and cannot control the process as it occurs. How can we decrease the variability among applicants and increase consistency of this selection method? We need to consider how the measure is administered.

Even if we have standard content for a selection method, dissimilarities in how we administer the selection methods result in extraneous factors possibly influencing the outcomes (and, ultimately, the quality of our selection decisions). Suppose that the interview in the example now contains a group of questions that the hiring committee uses for all applicants. When necessary, such as when we need to reinterview a candidate, when a previous applicant reapplies, or when we suspect the integrity of the items has been compromised, the committee accesses a repository of similar questions to draw on for the interview. Although the interview content is standardized, variations still occur in how it is administered. Suppose that the hiring committee is under pressure toward the end of spring hiring; the first applicants are given as long as needed to respond to interview questions, but the committee members soon realize that they need to restrict the interview time to one hour in order to process all applicants. They instruct applicants who are interviewed later in the process that they have seven minutes to answer each interview question. Time pressure represents an extraneous factor that affects some, but not all, applicants; applicants rushing their responses provide less detail and fewer examples in their answers, resulting in lower interview scores.

In the example of the teaching demonstration, although we exert less control over the content applicants upload, we establish specific instructions for applicants regarding the parameters of the demonstration, such as requiring that the demonstration depict the teacher interacting with students and include a clear demonstration of the methods used to convey subject matter. These directions structure the content for the selection method and also add to consistent administration of the method.

Standardizing the administration of the measure calls for ensuring that all applicants are given the same instructions, are given the same amount of time, and are asked to perform the selection assessments under the same conditions. Applicants who are required to interview in a stuffy room with no air conditioning in mid-July likely will perform differently than if they were interviewed in a comfortable environment. Similarly, the

order in which selection methods are used in the selection process might affect applicants' responses. Providing job simulation exercises before the interview might draw attention to
certain aspects of teaching deemed important by the school district. And prior exposure to the job simulation exercises primes
the applicants for interview questions; applicants who complete
the simulations after the interview receive no such benefit. Any
variation in the process used for collecting candidate information that potentially affects results should be identified and reduced or eliminated in order to be able to compare candidate
responses and make valid decisions about whom to hire.

Standardizing Scoring.   Standardizing content and standardizing administration serve as strong steps for improving selection systems, but they fail to account for a separate area in which
extraneous factors impact measurement: scoring, or the rules
we use for assigning numbers. Subjective measurement calls
for judgment. A number of factors, relevant and not, influence
judgment of job applicants. Reducing extraneous factors here
requires the organization to specify and agree in advance on
how scores will be assigned. Suppose that in the example each
interviewer rates the applicant on a scale for communication
skills (1 = poor communication skills, 3 = average communication skills, 5 = excellent communication skills). Although the
use of a rating scale represents an important step toward consistently scoring applicants, this rating scale allows undue influence by extraneous factors. First, each rater interprets the anchors differently; one interviewer comments to the others that
"no one is perfect, so I will not rate any applicant a 5." Another
interviewer defines the use of one verbal crutch (e.g., *um*), as
unacceptable and rates applicants who use one or more verbal

crutches as 1. Still another interviewer feels that simply answering the question constitutes "average communication skills," so the only way he assigns a 1 or 2 rating is if the applicant fails to answer. He justifies his approach by indicating that he doesn't want to upset applicants or discourage them from reapplying in the future, especially given the difficulty the district has in finding quality applicants. One meta-analysis of studies that involved observer ratings found that a substantial percentage of variance in ratings was due to raters' different interpretations of rating scales.[10]

Furthermore, the interviewers define the dimension of communication differently. One considers body language just as important as verbal expression. Others discount body language but pay attention to volume and articulation. Still another interviewer deems confidence applicants show in their responses as definitive of communication. These disparate definitions of communication affect the ratings the interviewers record; each interviewer attends to something different, and her ratings reflect these different emphases. Not surprisingly, the interviewers' ratings lack inter-rater reliability (see chapter 3). Although the interviewers witnessed the same event, their ratings differ markedly. In addition, the interviewers likely attend to novel features or behavior of the interviewee, and this influences ratings much more than is warranted. For example, researchers have found that participants in research studies tend to stare and attend more to physical differences in others when the participants feel certain that they are not being observed; however, they tend to work hard to ignore differences when they think another person will notice them staring. This early study documented the tendency for raters to attend to salient characteristics of individuals. Without clear criteria for evaluating applicants, raters could be drawn to salient, but irrelevant, applicant characteristics.[11]

Perhaps a similar lack of reliability occurs when the hiring committee members rate the videotaped teaching demonstration. Each rater defines effectiveness in a unique way and attends to distinctive facets of the demonstration (e.g., interaction with students or execution of the lesson plan). Furthermore, let's assume that no specific rating dimensions exist for the teaching demonstration, but it is evaluated in terms of "overall effectiveness." A plethora of plausible interpretations exist for effectiveness; we are reminded of the ongoing struggle for consistently defining teaching effectiveness (see chapter 2).

As these examples illustrate, a consistent scoring process is needed. Clear scoring rules should be established in advance of using a selection method. In our examples, unambiguous definitions of the dimensions (e.g., communication) structure the assessment so that interviewers or evaluators share a common idea of what they should attend to and evaluate. Furthermore, rating scale anchors warrant more detail, perhaps with examples for each rating (e.g., BARS), in order to truly anchor evaluators' responses. More detailed, behavior-based scales result in less rater error than do scales that require greater inference, such as a global assessment of personality.[12]

Specific instructions, clearly defined dimensions, and detailed rating scales help standardize scoring processes. However, another consideration for improving the accuracy of evaluators' ratings is to offer rater training. Rater training programs generally are used for improving performance appraisal systems; their purpose is to increase the accuracy, validity, and fairness of ratings.[13] They range from acquainting raters with the dimensions, rating scales, and other mechanics to methods for helping raters improve their observations and ratings.[14] Judicious use of rater training appears to decrease rater bias.[15]

Frame-of-reference (FOR) training is one of the better-known approaches to rater training, and it, of all rater training options, results in the greatest increases in rater accuracy.[16] It incorporates other approaches to training, such as emphasizing performance dimensions (performance dimension training) and providing examples of behaviors fitting certain ratings (behavioral observation training).[17] FOR training is intended to provide evaluators with consistent performance standards for each dimension.[18] Most research has focused on such rater training as a means for improving the accuracy of performance appraisal ratings, but the majority of published studies in the last few years apply FOR to other contexts, including selection.[19] Rater training contributes to standardizing the selection process when raters must rate performance against dimensions that require judgment.

FOR training teaches raters to use a frame of reference or a common perspective of performance when they observe and evaluate individuals.[20] First, trainees are tasked with rating work behaviors that relate to the job to see if their standards relate to the normative ratings made by others. Those with idiosyncratic standards are then given a job description and asked to rate performance against the job description of various ratees with different performance levels. They are then given the correct ratings for the behaviors, and the trainer and trainee discuss discrepancies. This practice and feedback help the rater identify which behaviors are important to observe, as well as define the standards against which each ratee should be evaluated.

Findings from a recent meta-analysis of FOR training effects found that trained raters were more accurately able to detect the strengths and weaknesses in ratees and could more accurately rank order them.[21] Furthermore, FOR trainees were able to make ratings more similar to those given by experienced raters, develop schemas (knowledge structures that help facilitate understanding and organize information) that resembled those of experienced raters, and demonstrate higher knowledge about the performance dimensions than those not participating in training.[22] These findings are particularly relevant for the selection process in which hiring decisions are made based on relative strengths and weaknesses.

Essentially, we have described ways to decrease the challenges evaluators face when making judgments about applicants using subjective methods. Consider the application of these approaches to scoring using the teaching observation example. Each member of our hiring committee likely holds a conceptualization of "teaching effectiveness" in mind against which performance on the observation is evaluated. These conceptualizations likely differ. We can attempt to get all evaluators on the same page, so to speak, by clearly articulating dimensions of performance and defining them. Offering evaluators behavioral-based or clearly defined anchors for rating scales will further standardize the process by reducing the likelihood of idiosyncratic ratings. However, we can boost accuracy by training the evaluators on how to rate the teaching observation consistently. This would be rather straightforward. Previously submitted videotaped teaching observations that varied in quality related to the dimensions could be chosen; evaluators could "practice" by rating candidate performance on these observations and then be given feedback on their ratings. With little effort, school districts could bolster the consistency and accuracy of subjective judgment, thus increasing the potential for more valid prediction of job success.

Districts that attend to standardizing measurement, administration, and scoring have completed most of the work toward the last point at which irrelevant information can taint selection: comparing applicants. Once a scoring process is standardized, it is relatively easy to compare across applicants and assume that the scores represent mostly the attributes we intend to measure rather than extraneous variables. However, even when we have carefully standardized other parts of the selection process, we must attend to the manner in which we compare applicants; we certainly don't want our hard work to be for nothing. For example, take a hiring committee that carefully evaluates candidates and begins comparing applicants to consider which to hire. One committee member remarks that Candidate A performed extremely well on the interview and recommends that he be hired; another committee member argues that Candidate B, who performed the best on the teaching observation, should be the choice; and a different committee member says that she just has a good feeling about Candidate C overall, that he just "fits in well" and should be hired. Had the committee identified initially a means for combining the data and determining the relative importance of the predictors, these problems would likely not occur. (Recall from chapter 8 the discussion of using multiple cutoff, multiple hurdle, or compensatory models for making decisions about candidates.) These decisions should be established before the selection process begins and then candidates should be evaluated against the system to determine which candidates will be offered jobs.

Here we have identified relatively straightforward improvements to create selection systems that will not tax the limited resources many districts face. Standardization represents the minimum a district should consider in making its current selection methods more valuable for identifying talent to hire.

II. BUILDING RESEARCH-BASED SELECTION TOOLS

The premise of this level of development is to build on the minimal investment approach of standardization by tapping new areas and improving applicant reactions. Standardization improves reliability and, by removing extraneous factors, enhances validity. That is, a clearer measure of the attribute and the removal of "noise" in our measurements afford us a better opportunity for making valid inferences about on-the-job performance from the data gathered during the selection process. In short, if our measures from the interview are based primarily on time pressure, practice effects, and interviewer attitudes, the "real" data of candidate performance gets lost; we instead make our decisions based on the influence of these extraneous variables, the noise. We suggest that a district build on the standardized system it has in place by identifying important competency areas that its current selection system fails to adequately measure.

Ideally, districts use a comprehensive test battery to cover the KSAOs that best predict performance. Often, this involves building a single tool and then moving to other selection tools as resources become available. To determine which tools to build first, start with a competency coverage grid that can be derived from the list of KSAOs discussed in chapter 2 or by adding to this list based on your district or school's unique characteristics. Competencies are combinations of KSAOs; they often distinguish levels of performance, and they serve as the basis for aligning HR systems.[23] Competencies are easier to use for selection than are traditional KSAOs because they often describe levels of proficiency; these can be used as the basis for structured interview rating scales or the criteria used for scoring other types of selection methods.[24] In addition, the use of competencies the hiring committee members are familiar with might make it easier to rate applicants; because competencies are couched in organizational language, they generally seem more job-related.[25] Furthermore, competency-based selection identifies what skills and experience candidates need for the short term as well as for the long term in order to benefit the organization.[26]

Some competencies might be gained through training or experience on the job; others needed prior to hire should be assessed using the selection system. To some degree, a selection system is deficient if it does not assess all of the important competencies needed on the first day of the job. The selection plan, or assessment plan, can be used to easily evaluate the current selection system on how well it's evaluating necessary competencies (see figure 9.1). The selection plan calls for listing the competencies relevant for a particular job, such as teacher, and then deciding whether each competency should be assessed during the selection process. It also lists the current selection methods. A grid is constructed so that competencies for selection are listed down the left side of the grid, and current selection methods are listed across the top. Each selection method is evaluated in terms of which competency or competencies it measures. Note that a competency is often measured by multiple tools.

The grid makes it easy to identify which competencies are not adequately measured by the current selection system. These

189

Figure 9.1

Sample competency selection tool grid

Teacher competencies	Teacher selection tool			
	Application	Teaching observation	Work sample/ simulation	Structured interview (phone)
Personal organization: The ability to manage time, prioritize, organize, and plan in order to accomplish work	✓		✓	
Interpersonal relationships: The ability to establish and maintain effective working relationships with others (e.g. teachers, administrative staff, parents, students)		✓		✓
Problem solving: The ability to analyze information and evaluate results in order to select the best solutions to problems	✓		✓	
Communication: The ability to share information with others in a clear and concise manner verbally and nonverbally; demonstrate respect and courtesy when communicating with others; and speak professionally		✓		✓

represent areas of deficiency in the system that could result in hiring teachers who simply cannot perform some of the essential job functions. It also detects selection methods that do not relate to the job competencies and selection data that have limited to no relationship to the job and therefore contaminate selection decisions. Using these data undermines the validity of other selection methods and could result in poor decisions about whom to hire.

Research in a number of settings illustrates processes for aligning human resource practices with each other and with the competencies required for the job in order to enhance the effectiveness of the organization. One study, conducted with a large southwestern U.S. school district, involved defining the competency model, establishing vertical alignment (how well each HR practice, such as selection, fits within the competency model), and establishing horizontal alignment (how well HR practices worked with each other in achieving organizational goals).[27] The district defined four domains as its framework for teaching: planning and preparation, the classroom environment, instruction, and professional responsibilities. These domains encompassed twenty-three components or competencies.

The district evaluated the selection process against these practice areas in terms of certification (whether state certification encompasses the competencies), assessment standards (the competencies of applicants), and hiring standards (minimum competency requirements for hiring). The average rating for how well these practices related to the competencies tended to be low, with the percent of vertical alignment ranging from 45 percent for hiring standards to 60 percent for assessment. Selection was estimated at 53 percent of alignment with other HR practices. Subject matter experts within the school district suggested changes to the current practices that would boost vertical and horizontal alignment. These suggested changes were then rated on their potential impact on teacher performance and how quickly they could be implemented (based on cost and difficulty of implementation). Grounded on their competency-based approach, the district found that its teacher selection system warranted immediate attention. The second-most-important priority recommendation, after improving performance management practices, called for improving the selection process by developing standard interview questions and response rubrics.

Using our competency grid, a district can determine which critical areas should be addressed by its selection system. From our experience, the following selection tools tend to offer a wide breadth of coverage across many types of competencies:

- Job simulations
- Short phone screen interviews
- Previous student test data
- Live interviews
- Teaching demonstrations (live or video)

Organizational members generally view competency-based practices favorably.[28] The relationship between the practice and the job is relatively transparent. In the example of the southwestern school district, competencies were used to develop interview questions and their rating scales.[29] Thus, selection practices look job-related and have high face validity.

Building New Tools

Once you have identified which tools to start with, use the appropriate chapter in this book to guide design decisions about how to level-up this aspect of your hiring process. By improving just one tool in-depth, the overall hiring decisions will be incrementally improved. When resources become available, additional tools can be improved. Often the most practical approach is to budget for improving one tool each year. By developing one tool at a time, a district can learn from early attempts and thus enhance the internal capacity (usually within HR) around effective hiring. In addition to developing each tool, it will be important to validate decisions made with the new tool.

Applicant Reactions

Applicants who perceive selection methods to have high face validity and believe those methods have high predictive validity tend to feel that the selection procedures and outcomes are fairer; they also have a more positive attitude toward the tests and selection.[30] Applicants perceive the selection methods that relate to the job in terms of content (i.e., interviews, work samples) more favorably than the methods in which the link to job content is less apparent (e.g., personality inventories, honesty tests). Thus, applicants view work samples and interviews as having greater face validity than do other selection methods.[31] Interestingly, applicants' assessments of scientific (not just face) validity appear accurate; in one study, they rated selection methods with more scientific validity more favorably.[32] In addition to considering face validity and scientific validity, applicants view more favorably the selection methods in which they feel they are given an opportunity to perform.

One consideration when adding and ordering selection methods is what applicants are expecting and how they will respond to each stage of the process. For example, researchers found that college students applying for jobs reported more positive reactions

during a selection process when they received prompt communication after the interview and had the opportunity to interact
with organizational members during a site visit.[33] Notably, they
found that recruitment information at one stage did not dissi-
pate by the next stage and that information received at a cam-
pus fair had a positive effect on attraction to the organization at
a later stage in the recruitment/selection process. Furthermore,
if the applicant experienced only one positive stage in the four-
stage recruitment/selection process, it was virtually the same as
having no positive stages; the researchers suggest that it might
take a number of positive experiences to overcome less positive
ones. One of the more negative combinations was a site visit in
which an applicant received only general information and had
very limited interaction with organizational members.

Similar findings have been found longitudinally within companies. In one study, researchers studied applicants applying for
a number of jobs in a large international publishing company.[34]
They examined the extent to which applicants' self-reported
senses of well-being and their attraction to the organization
differed as a result of how fair they perceived the selection system. For those hired, outcome fairness seemed more important
to their organizational attractiveness perceptions; for those rejected, procedural fairness seemed more important.

These findings suggest that structuring a selection system
on competencies needed for the job makes sense for organizational effectiveness and can also promote perceptions of fairness among job applicants. In addition, it's important to consider how applicants perceive the selection system: if applicants
feel they are informed during the process, have positive perceptions of each stage, and feel that the process and outcomes

are fair, they are more likely to react positively, even if rejected as a candidate. Positive applicant reactions can have substantive benefits related to future recruitment (when rejected candidates speak well of the district to other potential candidates), can improve incumbent impressions of new hires, and can increase the confidence of new hires that they were selected based on bona fide qualifications rather than extraneous variables. Other organizational outcomes have been cited as well. One researcher reviewed the plethora of literature on applicant reactions and proposed that applicant perceptions affect short-term outcomes such as impressions of the organization, behavioral intentions, and future performance on selection tools; longer term, these reactions might influence selected employees' actual behavior, job performance, and broader indicators of organizational success.[35]

III. EXECUTING A FULLY INTEGRATED HIRING SYSTEM

The premise of this level of development is to increase validity for the entire hiring process. Refining selection tools based on the district's population requires a substantial initial investment but saves time and money in the long run while improving results in a predictable way. Better validity often improves applicant reactions; in addition, valid selection measures are more legally defensible if challenged by unsuccessful applicants.

Here we describe customized validation studies at a high level and offer advice on how to use validation data to improve districtwide outcomes. We also discuss the various types of archival criterion data that might be available to schools (student test data from multiple tests, student grades, student ratings of teachers, performance evaluations, etc.) as well as newly created criterion measures (teacher observations, student rating forms, peer ratings, portfolio review for lesson plans, etc.).

As we discussed in chapter 3, validating a selection instrument is not as simple as marking it "valid" with a stamp. Instead, validation is a process of gathering and evaluating data that help us determine whether the method measures the attribute it intends to measure and how well it measures some outcome or criterion.[36] For example, you might establish that your structured interview measures the competencies or KSAOs that you consider essential for the teacher job. This would be evidence of validity. You also investigate and collect data showing that how applicants score on the interview relates to how well they perform as a teacher; those scoring higher on the interview have fewer complaints from parents and their classes have higher achievement scores. This also is evidence of interview validity. It's possible that a selection method measures some attribute but is unrelated to job performance. For example, you measure applicants' physical stamina, balance, and flexibility using a physical ability test. The test measures what it intends to measure—characteristics of physical ability—therefore, it's valid in that respect. Next, you investigate whether the applicants scoring higher on this test actually perform better as teachers. You find no relationship between physical ability test score and teaching effectiveness. Therefore, the evidence suggests that the physical ability test is not valid as a predictor of teaching performance. This doesn't mean that the test will not be valid as a predictor of job performance for other jobs; it could very well predict performance measures for police officers or firefighters.

Identifying Teacher Performance Criteria

In the above example, we were interested in predicting teaching performance, or teaching effectiveness. When considering validation, there might be a tendency to focus on the selection method with little thought given to outcomes. But we should actually begin our validation work by specifying criteria. Everything predicts something, but we want to make sure that we know which methods are or are not predicting outcomes that are important to the job. For example, how strongly someone prefers a brand of cola might predict certain outcomes in consumer behavior, but it is not likely to predict the important outcomes for a job as teacher.

Criteria have been defined as the standards that define job success.[37] It is unlikely, given the complexity of many jobs, that there is one ultimate criterion; rather, criteria tend to be multidimensional, and job performance dimensions tend to be independent of each other.[38] Subjective measures of performance often correlate weakly with objective measures of performance, suggesting that they measure different attributes.[39] We wouldn't, for instance, expect student grades on an objective exam to correlate strongly with supervisor's ratings of teacher effectiveness in preparing lesson plans. Additionally, overall performance might be considered from the perspectives of task performance versus contextual performance.[40] Task performance refers to the activities employees perform that contribute to the organization's technical core, while contextual performance encompasses organizational citizenship and prosocial behaviors that exist outside specific tasks (e.g., volunteering for committees). When making overall performance judgments about employees, supervisors generally weight each type of performance the same.[41] To the earlier point that selection methods will predict some criteria and not others, researchers found that a personality test was a stronger predictor of contextual criteria than of overall performance.[42] Therefore, the first significant challenge in examining the validation of teacher selection methods is to specify the criteria to be predicted.

Data for teacher performance already exists. These archival data might represent information related to student academic success, teacher behaviors and results, and other areas relevant for teacher performance. Student test scores (either national standardized or class-specific) represent student knowledge in the subject matter and could also be useful in determining the extent to which the teacher successfully conveyed the material to students, as can other student-centered data, such as students' evaluations of their teacher and the number of student/parent complaints against a teacher. Student grades, too, can be indicative of teaching effectiveness; students with higher grades presumably have more subject knowledge than do students with lower scores.

One could argue that these criteria are less than pure measures of teaching performance. These student-centered measures reflect some level of student knowledge or success (the attribute being measured), but they are also influenced or contaminated by various factors that are unrelated to student knowledge. For example, students might rate their teacher more favorably if he assigns them higher grades, so teachers might obtain higher evaluations not because they are more effective but because they are more lenient. Similarly, student grades might reflect leniency in order to portray the class as successful, whether or not the students have met knowledge or skill requirements. In addition, student test performance, while not necessarily subject to this leniency, might be less valid as a measure of student knowledge if the test content does not tap all of the content that defines the course's subject. Similar concerns exist for teacher-centered data. Performance evaluations completed on teachers could reflect rater bias by the principal, or the principal could lack the opportunity for making observations of teachers and, as a result, make generalized (and less accurate) assessments.

Try as we might, we will never have a perfect measurement criterion. However, we can evaluate how effective our criteria are by considering their relevance, sensitivity, and practicality.[43] First, the criterion should be related to the performance domain. It is clear that student test grades relate to the performance domain for the job of teacher, but it would be less clear how sales performance would relate to the teaching performance domain. The criterion also must be sensitive in that it discriminates between employees who are ineffective and those who are effective.

Suppose that we use seniority as a criterion that demonstrates performance. Some new teachers with one or two years on the job might be performing better than those with more years on the job. This measure doesn't clearly differentiate teachers' performance levels and would not be helpful as a criterion. Student scores on standardized assessments, however, might reflect which students were more prepared; if the better prepared students came from one teacher's class and the less prepared students were taught by a different teacher, the measure helps differentiate the teachers' performance levels. Finally, the criterion should be practical to measure and not interfere too much with the operations of the organization. For example, daily teaching observations would likely provide ample data to evaluate how effective teachers are; however, collecting data for this criterion would require substantial resource investment for the school district, could disrupt classroom culture, and would likely be opposed by teachers and other stakeholders (e.g., union representatives).

We might find the need to create new criterion measures as a way of adequately defining performance, especially if some critical parts of performance lack archival measures or reflect more bias than true performance on an attribute or if our existing criteria aren't relevant, sensitive, or practical. For example, an essential component of the teacher's job is to work with other teachers and school professionals in assessment and service activities. To measure this component, we might structure a peer rating measure so that teachers rate each other on their behaviors related to these activities. Suppose, too, that we recognize the limitations in students' assessments of teaching performance and decide to replace or supplement the existing student rating criterion with teacher observations, measuring teacher performance in the classroom quarterly to gauge effectiveness. Perhaps we also would prefer to get a longer-term measure of effectiveness, so we review teachers' portfolios and evaluate, using a standardized rubric, the effectiveness of those lesson plans.

All of these new criteria measures sound reasonable. However, there are certain steps that we need to take to develop these criteria.[44] First, we should conduct, or have access to, a job analysis. Next, we should develop measures that assess actual behaviors. Ideally, our next step would be to analyze the measures statistically (e.g., factor analysis) to identify criterion dimensions underlying the measures. This step most often involves an outside expert, except in the rare cases where a district has internal statistical expertise. In large districts these capabilities can sometimes be found in the evaluation/assessment department, and employees with these skills are likely to find this type of task a welcome variation from their typical work. In addition to analyzing the underlying constructs in the measures, we should perform reliability analyses for the measures (again, this will involve some statistical expertise). And finally, we should evaluate the selection methods based on their correlation to each criterion measure to establish predictive validity.

Content Validity

Once we build our criteria for defining teacher performance, we can examine the validity evidence for our current selection methods and any new methods we propose. A straightforward approach to examining validity evidence is to consider to what extent a selection method contains a representative sample of the content of a job. We heavily involve subject matter experts (e.g., teachers) in evaluating content validity. Organizations approach content validity in different ways. The approach we describe here is used with the Alabama State Personnel Department, and research has documented it as acceptable under the Equal Employment Opportunity Commission's *Uniform Guidelines* and as withstanding legal scrutiny.[45]

The State Personnel Department first conducted a job analysis to identify essential tasks needed on the first day of the job (minimum qualifications) and the KSAOs related to those tasks. SMEs then received a copy of the KSAOs and generated test items (interview questions) based on minimum standards. They were reminded to think of items relevant for someone who was new to the job and instructed to consider alternatives to the tasks (e.g., experience as an alternative to education). The minimum qualifications were articulated in a straightforward manner so that the SMEs could rate the interview questions in relation to minimum qualifications. Finally, the interview questions were mapped back to the KSAOs derived from the job analysis to establish their relationship.

While this example uses an interview, the same process would be used for any tool you're using in your hiring process. For instance, you could list all of the KSAOs your application form is designed to measure and ask SMEs to judge the relationship to the job.

Criterion Validity

Another approach to investigating the validity of a selection method is to link scores on the predictor/selection method with one or more criteria. This criterion-related validity approach is especially helpful if the content of the selection method looks unrelated to the job, such as when a veiled-purpose integrity test is used as one method for selecting sales representatives. To an applicant, it is unclear to what extent the questions on these tests relate to the job, such as "How often do you blush?" or "Are you an optimist?"[46] Most of the methods for selecting teachers (e.g., structured interview, job simulation, teaching observation), however, appear job related. Still, criterion-related validity is a good validation strategy because the approach calls for assessing how well each method predicts a performance criterion, not just how well the method samples job-related KSAOs.

Types of Criterion-Related Validity Studies. Criterion-related validation evidence can be gathered using either a predictive study or a concurrent study. A predictive study calls for using the selection method (e.g., new teaching demonstration) in the selection process for a group of applicants. Although data are collected on the new method, they are not used in the hiring decision; data are collected only for experimental purposes. Candidates are selected on the basis of the current system, or in some cases all candidates are chosen. At a later date the candidates, who are now employees of the organization, are assessed using the criterion measures. The candidates' scores on the new selection method are then correlated with their performance on the criteria as employees. This correlation represents the validity of the selection method in predicting the criterion. Sometimes, though, an organization must get a selection method in use as soon as possible and doesn't have time to conduct a lengthy study. A school district ramping up for spring hiring would want to ensure that a new selection method be implemented for screening large numbers of applicants, and having to wait until after the rush to implement a new selection method would pose an opportunity cost (e.g., missing the potential for hiring better talent).

A concurrent study requires less time to complete. In this type of study, current employees are asked to perform their best on an experimental selection method. Their performance is then scored, just as candidates' performance would be scored. The resulting predictor score is then compared against an existing performance criterion, such as performance appraisal ratings. The correlation between the predictor and the criterion represents the validity coefficient that serves as an estimate of how well the tool will predict job performance for future candidates.

Although the concurrent approach to criterion-related validity can be completed in a short period of time (sometimes within one day), its use poses some limitations. Current employees differ in their motivation level when taking a test, engaging in an interview, etc.; they have no incentive for doing their best, unlike the applicant who is hoping to obtain a job offer. In addition, the criterion measures might be those that currently exist rather than constructed specifically for the purpose of validation; thus, they might reflect some of the problems we specified earlier, such as bias. Finally, using existing employees in our study eliminates the lowest performers ("bad hires"), since these individuals already would have been screened out either through the selection system or through performance evaluation. Excluding lower performers restricts the range used for calculating the correlation, resulting in the correlation probably understating the strength of the relationship between the predictor and the criterion. Because of range restriction, the validity evidence we see for a concurrent-criterion study will always be lower than that from a predictive study.

Refining Selection Tools

Keep in mind that no perfect prediction exists and that our validity coefficients will not lead you to accurate decisions for all new hires. Even using the best available tools, you will inevitably make hiring mistakes. These "misses" or "bad hires" represent the inaccuracy of categorizing applicants in one group (will likely succeed on the job) based on their performance on the selection method and how their performance results differ from the initial assessment (they actually fail on the job). However, using selection methods with high validity coefficients and remaining selective in hiring will minimize these types of errors.

Some existing selection methods might show lower validity coefficients but could still benefit from major revision. Suppose a school district uses a structured interview. A criterion-related validity study shows that performance on the interview shows a lower correlation with teaching performance than expected. Rather than jettison the entire interview, the organization could evaluate the content of the interview, compare the content to the KSAOs or the competency grid, determine if rater errors exist and whether raters should be trained, and otherwise integrate structure into the interview to improve it.[47] It may be that only a portion of the interview is dragging down the validity, and revising just a few questions could improve things considerably. After having made the adjustments, validity could be reassessed to see if the changes did improve prediction.

Validity evidence helps a school district evaluate whether the time spent on the selection methods is worthwhile. If several methods are used and they have low validity in predicting important dimensions of performance, then the decisions made about applicants using these methods likely will be little better than random decisions. For example, an unstructured interview with a low validity requires substantial time and resources; teachers and the principal must appropriate valuable time to meet with the applicants and show them around the facility. However, the information they gain from the interview does little to help them select the candidate who will perform better than others. Of course, the district that dedicates this much time to selection and continues to hire lower performing teachers gets frustrated.

When validity coefficients for multiple predictors are compared, it might become apparent that two (or more) selection methods are predicting the same criteria in the same way. Statistical techniques can be used to determine if the methods are providing the same information or whether one is predicting something significantly different from the data from the other method. As with factor analyses and reliability analyses, these steps will require some specialized statistical expertise. If these analyses detect redundancy, one of the predictors can be eliminated, which would help streamline the selection process and save such resources as administration costs and staff time. A number of factors should be considered in making the decision to remove a predictor, among them determining which has more favorable reactions, which has the potential for less unlawful discrimination, and which is less expensive to administer.

Using thorough tools within the hiring funnel may require time investments by spending a little more time with candidates, but because the tools more accurately predict high performers, the time spent is a better investment as the funnel narrows. That is, as candidates pass through the hiring funnel, districts will spend a higher percentage of their time with more quality candidates. As it is now, principals likely see almost every candidate that is remotely plausible to hire based on their resume. By cutting out less-qualified candidates up front, principals spend more time with better candidates and end up with an overall higher-quality pool from which to choose.

Establishing validity evidence for selection methods strengthens an organization's defense against allegations of discrimination. Certain factors correlate more strongly with the potential for discrimination cases. For example, in one study researchers examined 371 court cases to identify which factors were more prevalent.[48] These researchers found that over a third of the cases occurred in public administration and government. Professional jobs accounted for 16 percent of the cases; 60 percent of these related to teaching jobs. Given the relative percentage of teachers to other professional job incumbents, the researchers concluded that "teachers would seem to be over-represented in terms of relative litigation rates."[49] Most cases (65 percent) had outcomes favoring the employer. The authors, however, suggest that teaching jobs might employ a multiple hurdle process in selection, and they propose that "if applicants are exposed to a greater number of tests, rejected applicants are more likely to perceive at least one of the selection devices as unfair or discriminatory."[50] They recommend that districts review their existing selection methods and eliminate or revise those with higher risk, such as the unstructured interview, and consider using those that were underrepresented in litigation, such as structured interviews and work sample tests. They suggest that the organization conduct a thorough job analysis and eliminate selection methods unrelated to the job, as well as conduct a validation study to identify unnecessary selection methods ("those that add little or nothing to the prediction of success for job applicants").[51] Furthermore, they recommend identifying whether two or more selection devices predict the same outcomes; if so, they recommended deleting those that are redundant, given that additional predictors that are unnecessary might increase the employer's exposure to litigation.

Making the Final Decision. The core premise of research-based hiring is investing resources in validation in order to identify and hire the best talent. No one wants to throw away validity at the last step in selection: hiring a new teacher. Using valid measures and then ignoring the scores, using only intuition to guide decision making, negates all the hard work validating the screening tools. Therefore, it's important to pay attention to the approach used to choose candidates for hire, whether top-down or rank order. However, some selection methods, such as cognitive ability tests, result in subgroup differences, particularly differences between racial groups. As such, top-down hiring with cognitive ability tests could result in districts hiring substantially fewer teachers from the lower performing subgroup. One way to address this issue is to group scores into bands. As mentioned in chapter 8, scores in a band or group are considered to be equivalent, though some care should be taken to make sure bands are created using samples of at least 150.[52] The use of bands is "based on the notion that small score differences may not be meaningful because they fall within the range of values that might reasonably arise as a result of simple measurement error."[53] Bands are most often used to help organizations achieve organizational goals for diversity while still making valid hiring decisions. In practice, organizations using banding treat all applicants in the band equally with regard to their qualifications for the job and then choose between members within a band based on affirmative action goals. In this way, a district can increase diversity of its teachers without compromising the integrity of the valid selection system.

SUMMARY

In this chapter, we suggest three levels of improvements that school districts can make, based on their available resources. While we recognize the reality of resource limitations for most school districts, we do recommend that all of these approaches be implemented in order to select teachers who will have the greatest potential for positively impacting the district. Our first suggested level of improvement in section 1 is that, at a minimum, districts should follow suggestions for standardizing their current selection system. As resources become available, additional work can be completed at the levels presented in sections 2 and 3. Level 2 improvements involve identifying untapped competency areas to assess with new selection tools, and level 3 improvements involve conducting and using validation study data to improve individual selection tools and thus improving the overall hiring process.

10

ADDRESSING CHALLENGES
COMMON TO SCHOOLS

Nothing can throw a wrench into a well-laid plan quite like actually implementing it. No matter how well organized a district is and well researched their hiring tools are, the hiring process rarely goes exactly as planned. The complexity of a school environment combined with the high volume of hiring makes it even more likely that something will go off course. In this chapter we address common, difficult circumstances that school districts face and share strategies for how to handle them most appropriately. While some of these best practices come down to applying common sense during stressful moments, common to all of our recommendations is a consideration of how a district's response to each circumstance will influence hiring.

The premise in each of our recommendations is that the screening tools in question are valid predictors of performance and that some research has been conducted to determine reliability, validity, and optimal passing scores. While it would be impossible to cover every possible difficult decision, we have tried to cover those we commonly see schools struggle with.

"I DON'T NEED THESE TESTS, I HIRE BY GUT"

School principals can make or break a school. A good principal sets the tone, upholds standards of behavior, and inspires students, teachers, parents, and community members toward the higher purpose of providing and supporting a great education. Principals can also be very persistent about how they want things done. Indeed, resilience can be an essential element of principal success. As such, it is quite common for principals (even the best of principals) to think that when it comes to hiring, they somehow have an inside track or an intuition for picking teachers who have "the right stuff" to excel in the classroom.

Unfortunately, "hiring by gut" doesn't always work. More precisely, hiring based on unstructured interviews or solely on the basis of resumes or even a past association ("I've known this teacher forever") will produce more hiring mistakes in the long run than using well-researched, structured screening tools. Hiring can be a bit like picking stocks: people will tell you about the great stock they bought that doubled in value a month later, but they rarely mention the three stocks that went nowhere or dropped in value. Likewise, principals will often remember their successes more than their failures and overestimate the accuracy of their decision making.

This circumstance highlights the value of local research on your hiring tools. If you have solid data illustrating the reliability and validity of your structured interviews, it will be far easier to demonstrate to principals how effective the tools can be. Then you can turn the tide and ask what research the principal has to prove her methods produce better results. In our experience, using policy and hard mandates is not as effective in the long run as showing the principals the value of using research-based tools. It is far better to engage the principals, involve them in building the tools, and then share the results with them. The carrot lasts longer than the stick. If you educate principals about the concepts, share the research, and make it clear that you are both working toward the same goal, they will use the tools and use them properly.

FAST-TRACKING APPLICANTS

One of the common requests during the hiring process will be to fast-track a particular applicant. This usually happens when someone involved in the hiring process (e.g., a principal, hiring manager, department chair) has past experience with a candidate or has a "desperate need" to fill a position quickly. The argument will be that the candidate has so much experience that he should be able to skip to the end of the process and just interview with the hiring school's principal (or whatever the final step might be).

Fast-tracking candidates creates a number of subtle problems. First, as we discussed in chapter 2, each screening tool covers only a small subset of the KSAOs needed to succeed as a teacher. A candidate who succeeds across the entire hiring process will have been tested on a meaningful and representative sample of all KSAOs needed to succeed as a teacher. If a candidate skips to the end, he will only be tested on attributes included in that particular screening tool. Imagine that a teacher excels at collaboration and is particularly adept at handling students who are struggling with material in a one-on-one setting. A principal

213

knows this about the candidate and insists on fast-tracking him to the final interview. As it turns out, the final interview covers the following attributes: collaborating with peers, handling difficult students, and listening skills. Not surprisingly, the candidate passes the final interview with flying colors and is hired. Unfortunately, the candidate did not complete the work sample or teaching observation portion of the overall process, and so his proficiencies on the attention to detail, writing lesson plans, and using classroom technologies KSAOs were never measured. This candidate may be hired and turn out to be a great one-on-one coach or learning specialist but have almost no ability to manage a classroom with a wide range of student abilities.

The second significant problem with fast-tracking is that it introduces personal bias into the overall hiring process. Fast-tracking necessarily relies on individuals' assumptions about a candidate that may be influenced by characteristics unrelated to performance as a teacher (e.g., race, sex, religious preferences, physical attractiveness, etc.). Without knowing it, the frequent use of fast-tracking could introduce systemwide bias into the overall hiring process.

Last, fast-tracking can have a significant long-term effect on the culture of a school and a school district. When fast-tracking is commonplace, it sends a message that some applicants are preferred or favored and that the best way to get hired is to know someone involved in the hiring process. Over the long term this can create a school culture that reinforces the belief that it's more important to know the right people than it is to do a good job. If a district is serious about improving educational outcomes at its school, the best course is the consistent use of screening tools that research confirms predict performance.

NO ONE PASSES

On very rare occasions, no one (or nearly no one) will pass a particular phase of the hiring process. More commonly, a district will realize that not enough candidates have made it through a particular phase given the number of hires needed. Consider the scenario where 92 teachers are needed, and from the 600 applicants, 390 make it through the initial application review to the second stage (phone interview). Of the 390 candidates screened by phone, the initial results suggest that only 100 passed. If there are two more steps in the process (say, teaching observation and final interview), then only 8 candidates will be screened out. In this scenario, the pass score for the phone screen has been set too high and needs to be adjusted to allow more candidates through the hiring funnel. Because recruiting pool base rates vary from year to year (see chapter 3), establishing and adjusting optimal pass scores for each screening tool is an inexact science that must be applied each year. While the process is inexact, it is essential to use some systematic methods to set the cutoff. While SMEs can be used in establishing an initial passing score for new screening tools, test score data (and validity research results) from current or past candidates should be used whenever possible.

The simple answer in this scenario is that when no one passes, a district must change the pass score to accommodate the proficiency level of the candidate pool. Remember that personnel selection is an entirely pragmatic exercise: it is about finding the *best* candidates from the *available* population. If a district has a subpar population of teachers from which to choose, then the only option (short of more recruiting) is to at least use valid screening tools to hire the best from those available.

AN APPLICANT IS EXCEPTIONAL IN SOME AREAS AND DEFICIENT IN OTHERS

It is likely that this scenario will appear in one of two variants. Scenario A is that you have an applicant with a rock star reputation and everyone is expecting her to perform exceptionally well during the selection process. She does perform very well on the phone interview (which confirms existing assumptions and bolster's confidence in her viability for the job), average on the teaching sample, and below average during her final interview with the principal. This is not what your selection committee expected. She has a reputation of stellar performance and great recommendations—what's happened?

Remember that when analyzing the job of teacher and designing the selection tools, take note of which KSAOs applicants need to possess before being hired and focus on these critical KSAOs when designing selection tools. If a particular KSAO can be trained or learned while on the job, then it wouldn't make a lot of sense to spend time measuring it in the selection process. So with this in mind, first you need to be certain that your selection tools are covering only those essential KSAOs that applicants must possess before hire. Unfortunately, if your selection tools are reliable and valid, and there are other candidates available who cleared all of the hurdles in your process, then you should pass on this candidate. While a large number of things could explain the unexpected results (e.g., poor PO fit, personal issues, etc), in the long run, the district will be better off for making data-based decisions.

In Scenario B, things are a little less black-and-white. An applicant scores incredibly high (close-to-perfect scores) on four of the selection tools (application, phone interview, teaching observation, final interview with principal) but then bombs on the work sample. Your principal and hiring committee love the applicant. She has stellar recommendations, and you were ready to hire her on the spot until her work sample scores were computed.

What do you do? This scenario will likely require you consider many things, among them:

- How badly do you want this candidate? Are her recommendations really that strong? How many other candidates in your pool do you believe are equally strong and who received higher scores?
- How important are the specific KSAOs measured by the failed selection tool to your organization? You should have a list of all KSAOs ranked in order of importance. Is this KSAO one of the top 5, or is it in the bottom 5?
- While, ideally, your selection tools should only measure those KSAOs required before hire, is it possible that this particular KSAO could be learned before the start date?
- Is it possible that there was some fluke in the process (e.g., during the work sample test the electricity went out, flustering the applicant) or that the applicant simply had a random personal incident that affected performance (e.g., ill, mishears the instructions)?

There is obviously a lot to consider and no right answer. You can always retest a candidate if you believe that his performance was hindered due to some outside factor(s). Retesting the applicant will give you data to defend his hire (assuming his scores improve) and perhaps provide some quality control over the process. But retesting applicants should be done only very rarely, when there is some clear indication that something went wrong with the initial testing. This solution should not be used as a standard approach, because it likely introduces considerable error into your overall hiring process. If this method is used too often, eventually internal political pressure will be used to trigger retesting for any candidate with connections to leadership or who is somehow a preferred candidate based on non-job-related bias.

A CANDIDATE CANNOT ANSWER AN INTERVIEW QUESTION BECAUSE OF A LACK OF EXPERIENCE

It is not uncommon that applicants for teaching jobs will either not have any prior teaching experience or will have not experienced the specific scenario referenced in an interview question. For example, an interview question might ask candidates about their experience leading a team of fellow teachers on a project. It's possible an applicant would have difficulty answering this question because she has never taught outside of student teaching training so hasn't worked with other teachers in a work setting or because she has worked on several teams with other teachers but was never the team leader.

While teaching-related experiences are obviously desired, you might be required to substitute for similar past experiences that measure the same KSAOs. For the teacher team leader question, you might have to ask the applicant to think about a time when she was in college and was the team leader for a project. If the applicant insists that she has never experienced that particular situation at any time in the past, you can ask her to think about how she would behave if that situation presented itself. Try to keep the question as close to the original interview question as possible, and make sure that your rating scale is still applicable. You will want to note on your score sheet that the candidate was asked a modified version of the original question. If this happens too frequently for a given applicant, you may need to score the interview as invalid and remove that candidate from the hiring process. If you anticipate a large number of inexperienced teachers in your applicant pool, it may be wise to shape your interview questions specifically to anticipate this possibility.

It is important to note that with applicants who do not have prior teaching experience, you should require a teaching sample from them. While your selection tools will be assessing the important KSAOs, there is no better predictor of performance than observing someone actually performing the job. In this extreme case, you will want to observe this applicant in the classroom before making a hire.

INTERVIEWERS DISAGREE ABOUT A CANDIDATE

The short answer to this problem is that if you stick to statistical scoring when combining interviewer ratings, the divergent views will average out. If interviewers become irrationally fixed on or against a particular candidate, you may need to recast the hiring committee and conduct another interview or simply exclude that interviewer's ratings. Alternately, you can use previous scores from earlier parts of the process to break the tie. While this is nicely objective, it does highlight the tendency for our preferences and subjectivity to creep in. Remind your hiring team that you are trying to be as objective as possible so that the interviewer(s) who did not get his preferred candidate will not take the decision personally. Also, a critical element of your training for interviewers should emphasize that they should be rating each response independently and be avoiding prejudging the candidates based on global perceptions about their suitability for the job.

WHEN THE CONTRACT GETS IN THE WAY

In unionized districts there is often a policy that when a position opens up, incumbent teachers can transfer from one school to the next due to seniority and regardless of performance. In effect, this transfer blocks other candidates who testing has predicted are likely to succeed on the job. When such transfers are allowed to happen—specifically, when the transferring teacher is not as skilled as the other candidate—overall district-level teaching quality will suffer. Of course, there are perfectly qualified teachers who transfer as well, and in these instances there will be no net effect on teaching quality at the district level. This particular element of labor agreements can have unfortunate, unintended consequences related to school culture, but there is rarely much that can be done to avoid it (except during contract negotiations).

In every case where we have worked with unions, we have found them to be very supportive of using valid selection processes. This is particularly true when the union can meet with researchers to understand the development and validation of the screening tools. We recommend sharing research results with the union and, where possible, involving its members in developing the instruments. Unions are motivated to have members who are high-quality teachers, and since the screening tools a district uses effectively select who will be in the union, they generally prefer valid tools over the other options. The other reason unions tend to prefer valid tools is they are, by definition, fair. The fundamental premise of any valid hiring process is that all candidates are treated equally, and generally this emphasis on fairness and transparency fits very well with the philosophy of organized labor.

CONFLICTS OF INTEREST AMONG INTERVIEWERS

There is always a possibility that an applicant is closely affiliated with an interviewer. A principal chooses to bring in applicants from her old school, or a family member applies for a position within the large school network. What's nice about using standardized, valid tools is that from the start they treat everyone equally. There is little opportunity for an interviewer with a conflict of interest to skip over a question he knows a particular applicant might have difficulty answering. But there is still the issue of perception, and we know all too well that perception is reality. In cases where there is a high potential for conflict of interest, it is best to remove the interviewer from that step for that candidate; ask a backup to conduct the interview and simply note why the backup was required.

A "PREQUALIFIED" CANDIDATE DOES NOT PASS ONE OR MORE STAGES

Some schools have contracts to accept a certain number of candidates from nationally recognized training or certification programs (e.g., Teach For America) that typically train strong teachers and send them to urban and rural schools for a predetermined number of years. Schools are often eager to receive these teachers and have employment agreements with

221

the organizations, agreeing to hire a certain number each year. You should treat these candidates exactly like your other applicants. You have spent a lot of time developing your selection measures, so stick with them and do the research so you know how much you can rely on your tools. Certifications have errors in them too, so believe the data that you collect more than the assurances of another organization. In addition to the essential KSAOs, you will also be assessing for how well the applicant fits with your school's individual culture and special characteristics.

SUMMARY

If your school is serious about improving educational outcomes, the best course is the consistent use of teacher screening tools that research confirms predict performance. While you should make your selection process as rigorous and scientifically sound as possible, it's still about people hiring people, and so there will be some pragmatic decisions to make along the way. While some flexibility may be necessary, the best way to improve the decisions you make is to build a top-notch process and then stick to it.

GLOSSARY

Behaviorally anchored rating scale (BARs). A type of rating system in which the rater or evaluator rates performance using a scale that shows typical examples of performance at various points on the scale. BARs use detailed labels at all or multiple scale points to provide better distinction between the scale points.

Behavioral description interviews (BDIs). A structured interview in which the interviewer ask candidates how they have addressed a situation in their past experience. The questions measure situations relevant to the job. These questions are past oriented in that they ask candidates to recount their experiences in dealing with a given situation; thus, they are appropriate for candidates with more extensive job experience.

Behavioral observation training. A method for training raters or assessors in which they are given examples of behaviors that fit various ratings on a rating scale. This type of training is used to increase inter-rater reliability by providing every assessor with a common understanding of how to interpret and apply the rating scale.

Compensatory models. Selection decision-making models in which a candidate's scores on various selection methods are combined.

A high score on one selection tool could compensate for a lower score on another selection tool.

Competency coverage grid. The combination of KSAOs into competency areas for a job that can then be compared to existing selection methods to ensure that all competency areas are adequately assessed during the selection process. This is a helpful visual aid that assists in ensuring that all critical competencies are being assessed by the selection tools.

Contamination. The extent to which a measure (assessment or test) includes information unrelated to what it was originally intended to assess.

Contextual performance. Activities employees perform that exist outside specific job-related tasks but that assist the organization, such as organizational citizenship and positive social behaviors (e.g., volunteering for a special holiday planning committee).

Correlation. A statistical relationship between two sets of data that shows how strongly the data (or variables) are related. Values range from –1.0 to +1.0, with values near 0 representing a weak relationship and values near –1.0 or +1.0 representing a strong relationship. Values closer to +1.0 indicate a positive relationship between the two sets of data (i.e., as values from the first data set increase, values from the second data set increase), and values closer to –1.0 indicate a negative relationship between the two sets of data (i.e., as values from the first data set increase, values from the second data set decrease).

Criteria. Outcomes that the organization is interested in predicting, such as performance, absenteeism, turnover, or counterproductive behavior.

Criterion-related validity. The extent to which a selection method predicts an outcome. This is measured with a correlation coefficient that indicates the strength of the relationship between the predictor and the criterion.

Deficiency. The extent to which a measure (assessment or test) excludes factors that are related to what it was originally intended to assess.

Error. Variables that decrease how well we measure a construct (e.g., job performance) or predict an outcome using a selection method. Error in measurement causes a test score to differ from a true level of competence. Error in prediction causes mistakes in identifying which candidates will be (un)successful on some job-related outcomes, such as performance.

Frame-of-reference (FOR) training. A type of rater training that calibrates raters so that they share the same concept of job performance. Raters generally are given experience rating a sample of videotaped job performance and then provided with feedback on the accuracy of their ratings. They are then given additional opportunities for rating, with feedback, until they hold consistent concepts of job performance. This type of training is used to increase inter-rater reliability by providing every assessor with a common understanding for how to apply ratings to the concepts they are measuring.

Hiring funnel. The concept of reducing the number of viable candidates using selection tools or methods. The number of applicants depicts the widest part of the funnel. Each selection tool reduces the number of candidates, so that far fewer (and ideally the best suited) are left when job offers are determined.

Incumbent base rate. The percentage of employees within a job who are successfully performing the job.

Internal consistency reliability. The consistency with which candidates respond to test items that measure a single construct. If a candidate answers the questions inconsistently, the test shows low internal consistency.

Inter-rater reliability. The consistency in ratings made of the same candidates by different raters or evaluators. A high inter-rater reliability indicates that the raters agree in their ratings of candidate performance on a selection method. A low inter-rater reliability indicates low agreement in how the candidate performed.

Item. A question on a test or selection method that is used to assess a construct.

Job analysis. A systematic process used for identifying the tasks and KSAOs needed to perform a job. This process involves the use of SMEs to help define the essential tasks and requirements of a job.

Job-related interviews. An interview in which the questions measure KSAOs related to the job tasks or requirements.

Job simulation tasks. Exercises or tests comprising a selection tool that simulate tasks that an employee would be required to perform on the job. One popular job simulation is the "in basket," where candidates are placed in a situation where they assume the role for which they are applying and perform tasks associated with that job.

Knowledge, skills, abilities, and other characteristics (KSAOs). KSAOs represent the requirements needed to perform the tasks of a job. Once the essential tasks are identified through a job analysis, the knowledge, skills, abilities, and other characteristics (e.g., personality, certification) needed to perform the tasks are identified.

Knowledge test. A test comprised of items that assess a candidate's familiarity with a body of organized factual or procedural information.

Multiple cutoff. A decision-making model in which candidates must exceed the cutoffs or passing scores of all selection methods in order to be considered for the job. Any candidate who does not meet the cutoff on one or more of the selection methods is rejected.

Multiple hurdle. A type of multiple cutoff approach to decision making in which selection methods are administered over time (not at the same time). Candidates must pass the first selection to move to the second, and so on. Those candidates who fail a selection method are rejected at that point in the selection process and do not move on to the next step.

Observed score. The score obtained from a test of a candidate's KSAOs. The observed score often differs from the candidate's true score of the construct because of error in measuring the construct.

Peer rating measure. A method for assessing performance that uses peers as raters or assessors.

Performance base rate. The percentage of employees who are successful performers.

Performance dimension training. A type of rater training in which raters are familiarized with the performance dimensions they will be using to rate employee performance.

Performance domain. The sum of all dimensions or factors that define performance for a specific job. One theory is that individual performance is made up of declarative knowledge (e.g., principles, facts, goals), procedural knowledge (e.g., physical skills, psychomotor skills, cognitive skills), and motivation (e.g., level of effort, persistence).

Person-job (PJ) fit. The extent to which a candidate's KSAOs fulfill the job requirements. A candidate with the required KSAOs will be more likely to successfully perform the job tasks.

Person-organization (PO) fit. The extent to which the candidate's values and characteristics (e.g., desire for teamwork) match the organization's values and culture.

Prediction. The process of using selection methods to estimate how well the candidate will perform on the job. Selection methods that are more accurate in predicting which candidates will perform well and which will perform poorly have higher validity.

Quality teaching. The extent to which teacher performance yields desired outcomes, such as student learning. More specifically, teaching practices should support children's learning of a broad range of cognitive, social, and specific academic skills.

Random error. A source of error or variability that affects candidate scores differently. This error stems from unsystematic or unpredictable sources.

Ratee. Individual whose performance is being assessed.

Rater. Individual assessing job candidates or employees.

Rater bias. The extent to which raters allow non-job-related variables to affect their ratings.

Rating rubrics. A standardized method of assessing candidate or employee performance that defines dimensions to be evaluated, provides a rating scale, and offers a method for scoring performance to arrive at an overall score. Sometimes also referred to as *scoring keys*.

Rating scale anchors. Definitions, often referencing observable behaviors, that are used to identify each level or point on a scale used to assess candidate or employee performance.

Reliability. The consistency of a measure. Consistency may be defined over time (e.g., test-retest reliability), within a measure (internal consistency), or in ratings made by different observers (e.g., inter-rater reliability).

Scoring key. A method for evaluating responses to items or questions and arriving at an overall score on the assessment.

Screening tool. Any tool, method, or instrument used for gathering data about applicants. Generally, screening tools refer to the methods used earlier in the selection process that help identify applicants who are obviously mismatched to job requirements.

Selection methods. Tools used to gather information about job applicants or candidates. The information gained from these tools is used for making hiring decisions. Examples include interviews and job simulations.

Selection/Assessment plan. A systematic approach to selection that involves identifying the KSAOs needed for a job, indicating which KSAOs should be assessed during the selection process, and then identifying which selection methods measure those KSAOs.

Selection ratio. The percentage of candidates hired from the number who apply. A small selection ratio means that the organization is selective in its hiring. A large selection ratio indicates that the organization is hiring more of the applicants who apply. The selection ratio ranges from 0 to 1.00. A selection ratio of 1.00 (or 100 percent) indicates that the organization is hiring every applicant who applies. The selection ratio is also referred to as *selection rate*.

Selection tool. Any method or instrument used to gather information about job candidates. This information is used in making decisions about which candidate(s) to hire. Examples include resumes, interviews, and job simulations.

Situational interviews (SIs). A structured interview in which the questions outline possible situations a candidate might encounter on the job. The candidate responds with how she would address the issue. These questions are future oriented in that they ask the candidates how they would perform given the job-related situation; thus, they are appropriate for candidates with little or no job experience.

Standardization. A process in which measurement error is reduced by having a test or method administered and used consistently.

Standardized rating scales. Scales used for evaluating candidate performance on questions or tests that are well defined and consistently used across evaluators.

Structured interview. A selection technique used for gathering information from job candidates that involves asking the same set of questions across all candidates. The questions relate to the job requirements, and the interview process is standardized.

Subject matter experts (SMEs). Individuals often consulted during job analysis who have expertise about job requirements. Typically, high performing individuals in a job are selected to serve as SMEs during a job analysis.

Systematic error. A source of error or variability that affects all candidate scores similarly. This variability comes from predictable factors.

Systematic variance. Consistent or predictable differences in candidate scores. These differences come from predictable factors, such as candidates' differences in true scores, as well as systematic error.

Task performance. Job-related tasks or activities that employees perform that contribute to the organization's technical core.

Teacher quality. The extent to which the teacher meets job requirements and accomplishes expected performance outcomes.

True score. The actual level of a construct (e.g., knowledge) that a candidate possesses. This may differ from an observed score obtained on a test of the construct.

Unstructured interview. A selection technique used for gathering information from candidates that involves asking questions. Questions often differ across candidates and may not have a connection to job requirements. Generally no standardized rating scale is used for evaluating responses.

Validity. The extent to which a selection method or tool measures what it intends to measure and predicts a practical criterion or outcome, such as performance, absenteeism, or turnover.

Validity coefficient. A value, usually a correlation, that represents the validity of a selection method. Usually this value designates how well the selection method predicts some criterion, or outcome. Validity coefficients near 0 represent a weak relationship between the selection method (predictor) and outcome/criterion (e.g., job performance). A validity coefficient of (+/–) .3 or higher represents a strong relationship between the predictor and the criterion.

Work samples. A selection tool or method that involves having candidates submit samples of their work (e.g., a portfolio) or perform a task that would be required of them on the job (similar to a job simulation).

NOTES

Chapter I

1. Frank L. Schmidt and John E. Hunter, "The Validity and Utility of Selection Methods in Personnel Psychology: Practical and Theoretical Implications of 85 Years of Research Findings," *Psychological Bulletin* 124, no. 2 (1998): 262–274.

2. "State Teacher Policy Yearbook" (Washington, DC: National Council on Teacher Quality, 2008).

3. Jason Song, "Firing Teachers Can Be a Costly and Tortuous Task," *Los Angeles Times,* May 3, 2009.

4. Ericka Mellon, "Houston Independent School District Policy Puts Hiring to the Test: Grier's Tougher Standards Strain Recruiting as Fall Posts Open Up," *Houston Chronicle,* June 20, 2010.

5. Patricia Buckley Ebrey, *The Cambridge Illustrated History of China,* 2nd ed. (Cambridge, UK: Cambridge University Press, 2010), 145–147, 198–200.

6. "China's Civil Service Selection Examination," eTeacher Chinese Official Blog, http://blog.eteacherchinese.com/uncategorized/chinas-civil-service-selection-examination.

7. Fredrick P. Morgeson and Erich C. Dierdorff, "Work Analysis: From Technique to Theory," in *APA Handbook of Industrial and Organizational Psychology,* vol. 2, ed. Sheldon Zedeck (Washington, DC: American Psychological Association, 2011), 3–41

8. Andrew English and Christine Thomas, *Development and Validation of a Test Battery for Pre-Employment Selection of Teachers at Uplift Education* (Emeryville, CA: 3D Group, 2010).

9. Allen I. Huffcut and Winfred Arthur, "Hunter and Hunter (1984) Revisited: Interview Validity for Entry-Level Jobs," *Journal of Applied Psychology* 79, no. 2 (1994): 184–190.

10. Wayne Cascio, *Applied Psychology in Personnel Management* (Englewood Cliffs, NJ: Prentice Hall, 2001).

11. Steven G. Rivkin, Eric A. Hanushek, and John F. Kain, "Teachers, Schools, and Academic Achievement" (Washington, DC: National Bureau of Economic Research, 2001).

12. Eric A. Hanushek, "Teacher Deselection," in *Creating a New Teaching Profession,* ed. Dan Goldhaber and Jane Hannaway (Washington, DC: Urban Institute Press, 2009), 165–180.

13. Frank Eltman, "Firing Tenured Teachers Isn't Just Difficult, It Costs You," *USA Today,* June 30, 2008, http://usatoday30.usatoday.com/news/education/2008-06-30-teacher-tenure-costs_N.htm.

14. Ben Chapman, "Troubled City Teachers Still Bouncing Around the Supposedly Shutdown 'Rubber Rooms' as City Wastes $22 Million a Year," *New York Daily News,* October 16, 2012.

15. Eric A. Hanushek, "Valuing Teachers: How Much Is a Good Teacher Worth?" *Education Next* 11, no. 3 (2011): 40–45.

Chapter 2

1. Jerome A. Cranston, "Evaluating Prospects: The Criteria Used to Hire New Teachers," *Alberta Journal of Educational Research* 58, no. 3 (2012): 350–367; Stacey A. Rutledge, Douglas N. Harris, Cynthia T. Thompson, and W. Kyle Ingle, "Certify, Blink, Hire: An Examination of the Process and Tools of Teacher Screening and Selection," *Leadership and Policy in Schools* 7, no. 3 (2008): 258.

2. Jane Ziebarth-Bovill, Jeff Kritzer, and Ronald Bovill, "The Essential Criteria for Hiring First Year Teacher Candidates," *Education* 133, no. 1 (2012): 125–138.

3. Jerome A. Cranston, "Evaluating Prospects: The Criteria Used to Hire New Teachers," *Alberta Journal of Educational Research* 58, no. 3 (2012): 350–367.

4. Richard W. Mason and Mark P. Schroeder, "Principal Hiring Practices: Toward a Reduction of Uncertainty," *The Clearing House* 83, no. 5 (2010): 186–193.

5. Ibid.

6. Stacey A. Rutledge, Douglas N. Harris, and William K. Ingle, "How Principals 'Bridge and Buffer' the New Demands of Teacher Quality and Accountability: A Mixed-Methods Analysis of Teacher Hiring," *American Journal of Education* 116, no. 2 (2010): 211–241.

7. Linda Darling-Hammond, "Teacher Quality and Student Achievement: A Review of State Policy Evidence," *Education Policy Analysis Archives* 8, no. 1 (2000): 1–44.

8. Marcus A. Winters, Bruce L. Dixon, and Jay P. Greene, "Observed Characteristics and Teacher Quality: Impacts of Sample Selection on a Value Added Model," *Economics of Education Review* 31, no. 1 (2012): 19–32.

9. Scott Alan Metzger and Meng-Jia Wu, "Commercial Teacher Selection Instruments: The Validity of Selecting Teachers Through Beliefs, Attitudes, and Values," *Review of Educational Research* 78, no. 4 (2008): 921–940.

10. Ibid.

11. Rutledge, Harris, Thompson, and Ingle, "Certify, Blink, Hire," 237–263.

12. Ibid., 258.

13. Edward L Levine, *Everything You Always Wanted to Know About Job Analysis* (Temple Terrace, FL: Mariner, 1983).

14. 3D Group, *Teacher Job Analysis Report*, 3D Group Technical Report No. 8332 (Berkeley, CA: 3D Group, 2010).

15. Ibid.

16. Robert G. Croninger, Daria Buese, and John Larson, "A Mixed-Methods Look at Teaching Quality: Challenges and Possibilities from One Study," *Teachers College Record* 114, no. 4 (2012): 1–36.

17. Linda Darling-Hammond, "Recognizing and Enhancing Teacher Effectiveness," The *International Journal of Educational and Psychological Assessment* 3 (December 2009): 2.

18. Ibid., 3.

19. Howard Ebmeier and Jennifer Ng, "Development and Field Test of an Employment Selection Instrument for Teachers in Urban School Districts," *Journal of Personnel Evaluation in Education* 18, no. 3 (2005): 201–218.

20. Amy L. Kristof-Brown, Ryan D. Zimmerman, and Erin C. Johnson, "Consequences of Individuals' Fit at Work: A Meta-Analysis of

Person-Job, Person-Organization, Person-Group, and Person-Supervisor Fit," *Personnel Psychology* 58, no. 2 (2005): 281–342.

21. Ibid.
22. Rutledge, Harris, Thompson, and Ingle, "Certify, Blink, Hire," 258.

Chapter 3

1. Stacey A. Rutledge, Douglas N. Harris, Cynthia T. Thompson, and W. Kyle Ingle, "Certify, Blink, Hire: An Examination of the Process and Tools of Teacher Screening and Selection," *Leadership and Policy in Schools* 7 (2008): 237–263.
2. Jum C. Nunnally, *Psychometric Theory* (New York: McGraw Hill, 1978).
3. Lee J. Cronbach et al., *The Dependability of Behavioral Measurements: Theory of Generalizability for Scores and Profiles* (New York: Wiley, 1972).
4. Ibid.
5. Robert M. Guion, "Validity and Reliability," in *Handbook of Research Methods in Industrial and Organizational Psychology*, ed. Steven G. Rogelberg (Malden: MA: Blackwell, 2002), 57–76.
6. Ibid., 70.
7. Robert R. McCrae and Paul T. Costa, "Self-Concept and the Stability of Personality: Cross-Sectional Comparisons of Self-Reports and Ratings," *Journal of Personality and Social Psychology* 43, no. 6 (1982): 1282–1292.
8. Lee J. Cronbach, "Test Validation," in *Educational Measurement,* 2nd ed., ed. Robert L. Thorndike (Washington, DC: American Council on Education, 1971), 443–507.
9. Samuel Messick, "Validity," in *Educational Measurement*, 3rd ed., ed. Robert L. Linn (New York: Macmillan, 1989), 13–103.
10. Kevin R. Murphy and Charles O. Davidshofer, *Psychological Testing* (Englewood Cliffs, NJ: Prentice-Hall), 137.
11. Jerome A. Cranston, "Evaluating Prospects: The Criteria Used to Hire New Teachers," *Alberta Journal of Educational Research* 58, no. 3 (2012): 350–367; Richard W. Mason and Mark P. Schroeder, "Principal Hiring Practices: Toward a Reduction of Uncertainty," *The Clearing House* 83, no. 5 (2010): 186–193.
12. Michael A. McDaniel et al., "The Validity of Employment Interviews: A Comprehensive Review and Meta-Analysis," *Journal of Applied Psychology* 79, no. 4 (1994): 599–616.

13. Michael A. Campion, James E. Campion, and J. Peter Hudson Jr., "Structured Interviewing: A Note on Incremental Validity and Alternative Question Types," *Journal of Applied Psychology* 79, no. 6 (1994): 998–1002

14. McDaniel et al., "The Validity of Employment Interviews."

15. Christopher Orpen, "Patterned Behavior Description Interviews versus Unstructured Interviews: A Comparative Validity Study," *Journal of Applied Psychology* 70, no. 4 (1985): 774–776.

16. Ken Emley and Howard Ebmeier, "The Effect of Employment Interview Format on Principals' Evaluations of Teachers," *Journal of Personnel Evaluation in Education* 11, no. 1 (1997): 39–56.

17. Jennifer Hindman and James Stronge, "The $2 Million Decision: Teacher Selection and Principals' Interviewing Practices," *ERS Spectrum* 27, no. 3 (2009): 1–10.

18. Willi H. Wiesner and Steven F. Cronshaw, "A Meta-Analytic Investigation of the Impact of Interview Format and Degree of Structure on the Validity of the Employment Interview," *Journal of Occupational Psychology* 61, no. 1 (1988): 275–290.

19. McDaniel et al., "The Validity of Employment Interviews."

20. Ibid.

21. Hindman and Stronge, "The $2 Million Decision."

22. James J. Asher and James A. Sciarrino, "Realistic Work Sample Tests: A Review," *Personnel Psychology* 27, no. 5 (1974): 319–533.

23. C. J. Vincent, C. Montecinos, and R. Boody, "Using the Beginning Teacher Professional Portfolio in the Employment Process," *Journal of Employment in Education* 1, no. 1 (1997): 33–43.

24. Robert M. Boody, "Career Services Perspectives on the Use of Portfolios in the Teacher Employment Process: A Survey," *Education* 30, no. 1 (2009): 67–71.

25. Edward Liu and Susan Moore Johnson, "New Teachers' Experiences of Hiring: Late, Rushed, and Information-Poor," *Educational Administration Quarterly* 42, no. 3 (2006): 324–360.

26. Rutledge, Harris, Thompson, and Ingle, "Certify, Blink, Hire."

27. Frank L. Schmidt and John E. Hunter, "The Validity and Utility of Selection Methods in Personnel Psychology: Practical and Theoretical Implications of 85 Years of Research Findings," *Psychological Bulletin* 124, no. 2 (1998): 262–274.

28. Paul R. Sackett, Neil Schmitt, Jill E. Ellingson, and Melissa B. Kabin, "High-Stakes Testing in Employment, Credentialing, and Higher Education: Prospects in a Post Affirmative-Action World," *American Psychologist* 56, no. 4 (2001): 302–318.
29. Ibid.
30. Frank L. Schmidt et al., "Job Sample vs. Paper-and-Pencil Trades and Technical Tests: Adverse Impact and Examinee Attitudes." *Personnel Psychology* 30, no. 2 (1977): 187–197.
31. Schmidt and Hunter, "The Validity and Utility of Selection Methods in Personnel Psychology."
32. Richard W. Mason and Mark P. Schroeder, "Principal Hiring Practices: Toward a Reduction of Uncertainty," *The Clearing House* 83, no. 5 (2010): 186–193.
33. Ibid.
34. Ibid.
35. Jerome A. Cranston, "Evaluating Prospects: The Criteria Used to Hire New Teachers," *Alberta Journal of Educational Research* 58, no. 3 (2012): 350–367.
36. Ibid.
37. Ibid.
38. Ibid.
39. Mason and Schroeder, "Principal Hiring Practices."

Chapter 4

1. K. D. Peterson, *Effective Teacher Hiring: A Guide to Getting the Best* (Alexandria, VA: Association of Supervision and Curriculum Development, 2002).
2. A. J. Bolz, "Screen Teacher Candidates: Luck of the Draw or Objective Selection" (Ph.D. dissertation, University of Wisconsin, Madison, 2009).
3. Richard W. Mason and Mark P. Schroeder, "Principal Hiring Practices: Toward a Reduction of Uncertainty," *The Clearing House* 83, no. 5 (2010): 186–193.
4. Ericka Mellon, "Houston Independent School District Policy Puts Hiring to the Test: Grier's Tougher Standards Strain Recruiting as Fall Posts Open Up," *Houston Chronicle*, June 20, 2010.

Chapter 5

1. Lee. J. Cronbach, *Essentials of Psychological Testing*, 2nd ed. (New York: Harper & Row, 1960), 457.
2. Paul F. Wernimont and John P. Campbell, "Signs, Samples, and Criteria," *Journal of Applied Psychology* 52, no. 5 (1968): 372–376.
3. Robert Wood, "Work Samples Should Be Used More (and Will Be)," *International Journal of Selection and Assessment* 2, no. 3 (1994): 166.
4. Wernimont and Campbell, "Signs, Samples, and Criteria," 373.
5. James J. Asher and James A. Sciarrino, "Realistic Work Sample Tests: A Review," *Personnel Psychology* 27, no. 4 (1974): 519–533.
6. Frank L. Schmidt and John E. Hunter, "The Validity and Utility of Selection Methods in Personnel Psychology: Practical and Theoretical Implications of 85 Years of Research Findings," *Psychological Bulletin* 124, no. 2 (1998): 262–274.
7. James E. Campion, "Work Sampling for Personnel Selection," *Journal of Applied Psychology* 56, no. 1 (1972): 40–44.
8. Herbert G. Heneman III and Timothy A. Judge, *Staffing Organizations*, 6th ed. (New York: McGraw-Hill).
9. John E. Hunter and Ronda F. Hunter, "Validity and Utility of Alternative Predictors of Job Performance," *Psychological Bulletin* 96, no. 1 (1984): 72–98.
10. Ibid.; Schmidt and Hunter, "The Validity and Utility of Selection Methods in Personnel Psychology."
11. Ivan T. Robertson and R. S. Kandola, "Work Sample Tests: Validity, Adverse Impact and Applicant Reaction," *Journal of Occupational Psychology* 55, no. 3 (1982): 171–183.
12. James J. Asher and James A. Sciarrino, "Realistic Work Sample Tests: A Review," *Personnel Psychology* 27, no. 4 (1974): 519–533; James E. Campion, "Work Sampling for Personnel Selection," *Journal of Applied Psychology* 56, no. 1 (1972): 40–44.
13. Militza Callinan and Ivan T. Robertson, "Work Sample Testing," *International Journal of Selection and Assessment* 8, no. 4 (2000): 256.
14. Asher and Sciarrino, "Realistic Work Sample Tests."
15. Ibid.
16. Robertson and Kandola, "Work Sample Tests."
17. Ibid.
18. Philip L. Roth, Philip Bobko, and Lynn A. McFarland, "A Meta-Analysis of Work Sample Test Validity: Updating and Integrating

Some Classic Literature," *Personnel Psychology* 58, no. 4 (2005): 1009–1037.

19. Wood, "Work Samples Should Be Used More (and Will Be)."

20. Stephan J. Motowidlo, Marvin D. Dunnette, and Gary W. Carter, "An Alternative Selection Procedure: The Low-Fidelity Simulation," *Journal of Applied Psychology* 75, no. 6 (1990): 640–647.

21. Ibid.

22. Filip Lievens and Fiona Patterson, "The Validity and Incremental Validity of Knowledge Tests, Low-Fidelity Simulations, and High-Fidelity Simulations for Predicting Job Performance in Advanced-Level High-Stakes Selection," *Journal of Applied Psychology* 96, no. 5 (2011): 927–940.

23. Callinan and Robertson, "Work Sample Testing."

24. Wood, "Work Samples Should Be Used More (and Will Be)."

25. Motowidlo, Dunnette, and Carter, "An Alternative Selection Procedure."

26. Deborah L. Whetzel and Michael A. McDaniel, "Situational Judgment Tests: An Overview of Current Research," *Human Resource Management Review* 19, no. 3 (2009): 188–202.

27. Filip Lievens and Fiona Patterson, "The Validity and Incremental Validity of Knowledge Tests, Low-Fidelity Simulations, and High-Fidelity Simulations for Predicting Job Performance in Advanced-Level High-Stakes Selection," *Journal of Applied Psychology* 96, no. 5 (2011): 927–940.

28. Motowidlo, Dunnette, and Carter, "An Alternative Selection Procedure: The Low-Fidelity Simulation," *Journal of Applied Psychology* 75, no. 6 (1990): 640–647.

29. Paul R. Sackett et al., "High-Stakes Testing in Employment, Credentialing, and Higher Education: Prospects in a Post-Affirmative-Action World," *American Psychologist* 56, no. 4 (2001): 310.

30. Diana L. Deadrick and Donald G. Gardner, "Maximal and Typical Measures of Job Performance: An Analysis of Performance Variability Over Time," *Human Resource Management Review* 18, no. 3 (2008): 133–145.

31. Robert M. Boody, "Career Services Perspectives on the Use of Portfolios in the Teacher Employment Process: A Survey," *Education* 130, no. 1 (2009): 67–71.

32. Jerome A. Cranston, "Evaluating Prospects: The Criteria Used to Hire New Teachers," *Alberta Journal of Educational Research* 58, no. 3 (2012): 350–367.
33. Richard W. Mason and Mark P. Schroeder, "Principal Hiring Practices: Toward a Reduction of Uncertainty," *The Clearing House* 83, no. 5 (2010): 186–193.
34. Stacey A. Rutledge, Douglas N. Harris, Cynthia T. Thompson, and W. Kyle Ingle, "Certify, Blink, Hire: An Examination of the Process and Tools of Teacher Screening and Selection," *Leadership and Policy in Schools* 7, no. 3 (2008): 237–263.
35. Ibid.
36. Wood, "Work Samples Should Be Used More (and Will Be)."
37. Frank L. Schmidt, John E. Hunter, and Alice N. Outerbridge, "Impact of Job Experience and Ability on Job Knowledge, Work Sample Performance, and Supervisory Ratings of Job Performance," *Journal of Applied Psychology* 71, no. 3 (1986): 432–439.
38. Robertson and Kandola, "Work Sample Tests."
39. Callinan and Robertson, "Work Sample Testing."
40. Wood, "Work Samples Should Be Used More (and Will Be)."
41. Ibid.
42. Walter C. Borman and Glenn L. Hallam, "Observation Accuracy for Assessors of Work-Sample Performance: Consistency Across Task and Individual-Differences Correlates," *Journal of Applied Psychology* 76, no. 1 (1991): 11–18.
43. Ibid.
44. Leaetta M. Hough, Margaret A. Keyes, and Marvin D. Dunnette, "An Evaluation of Three 'Alternative' Selection Procedures," *Personnel Psychology* 36, no. 2 (1983): 261–276; Paul G. LeMahieu, Drew H. Gitomer, and JoAnne Eresh, "Portfolios in Large-Scale Assessment: Difficult but Not Impossible," *Educational Measurement: Issues and Practice* 14, no. 3 (1995): 11–16, 25–28.

Chapter 6

1. Frank L. Schmidt and Ryan D. Zimmerman, "A Counterintuitive Hypothesis about Employment Interview Validity and Some Supporting Evidence," *Journal of Applied Psychology* 89, no. 3 (2004): 553–561.

2. Richard W. Mason and Mark P. Schroeder, "Principal Hiring Practices: Toward a Reduction of Uncertainty," *The Clearing House* 83, no. 5 (2010): 196–193; Stacey A. Rutledge, Douglas N. Harris, Cynthia T. Thompson, and W. Kyle Ingle, "Certify, Blink, Hire: An Examination of the Process and Tools of Teacher Screening and Selection," *Leadership and Policy in Schools* 7, no. 3 (2008): 237–263.

3. Michael A. McDaniel, Deborah L. Whetzel, Frank L. Schmidt, and Steven D. Maurer, "The Validity of Employment Interviews: A Comprehensive Review and Meta-Analysis," *Journal of Applied Psychology* 79, no. 4 (1994): 599–616.

4. Gary P. Latham, Lise M. Saari, Elliott D. Pursell, and Michael A. Campion, "The Situational Interview," *Journal of Applied Psychology* 65, no. 4 (1980): 422–427.

5. Tom Janz, "Initial Comparisons of Patterned Behavior Description Interviews versus Unstructured Interviews," *Journal of Applied Psychology* 67, no. 5 (1982): 577–580.

6. McDaniel, Whetzel, Schmidt, and Maurer, "The Validity of Employment Interviews."

7. Ibid.

8. Ibid.

9. Latham, Saari, Pursell, and Campion, "The Situational Interview."

10. Tom Janz, "Initial Comparisons of Patterned Behavior Description Interviews versus Unstructured Interviews," *Journal of Applied Psychology* 67, no. 5 (1982): 577–580.

11. Michael A. Campion, James E. Campion, and J. Peter Hudson, Jr., "Structured Interviewing: A Note on Incremental Validity and Alternative Question Types," *Journal of Applied Psychology* 79, no. 6 (1994): 998–1002.

12. Allen I. Huffcutt, James M. Conway, Philip L. Roth, and Ute-Christine Klehe, "The Impact of Job Complexity and Study Design on Situational and Behavior Description Interview Validity," *International Journal of Selection and Assessment* 12, no. 3 (2004): 262–273.

13. Gerard H. Seijts and Ivy Kyei-Poku, "The Role of Situational Interviews in Fostering Positive Reactions to Selection Decisions," *Applied Psychology: An International Review* 59, no. 3 (2010): 431–453.

14. McDaniel, Whetzel, Schmidt, and Maurer, "The Validity of Employment Interviews."

15. Michael A. Campion, David K. Palmer, and James E. Campion, "Structuring Employment Interviews to Improve Reliability, Validity, and Users' Reactions," *Current Directions in Psychological Science* 7, no. 3 (1998): 77–82.

16. Murray R. Barrick, Brian W. Swider, and Greg L. Stewart, "Initial Evaluations in the Interview: Relationships with Subsequent Interviewer Evaluations and Employment Offers," *Journal of Applied Psychology* 95, no. 6 (2010): 1163–1172.

17. Ibid.; Murray R. Barrick et al., "Candidate Characteristics Driving Initial Impressions During Rapport Building: Implications for Employment Interview Validity," *Journal of Occupational and Organizational Psychology* 85, no. 2 (2012): 330–352.

18. Allen I. Huffcutt, "An Empirical Review of the Employment Interview Construct Literature," *International Journal of Selection and Assessment* 19, no. 1 (2011): 62–81.

19. For a review of relevant literature, see Michael A. Campion, David K. Palmer, and James E. Campion, "A Review of Structure in the Selection Interview," *Personnel Psychology* 50, no. 3 (1997): 655–702.

20. Ibid.

21. Michael A. Campion, Elliott D. Pursell, and Barbara K. Brown, "Structured Interviewing: Raising the Psychometric Properties of the Employment Interview," *Personnel Psychology* 41, no. 1 (1988): 25–42.

22. Andrew English and Christine Thomas, *Development and Validation of a Test Battery for Pre-Employment Selection of Teachers at Uplift Education,* Technical Report No. 8332 (Emeryville, CA: Data Driven Decisions, 2010).

23. Campion, Palmer, and Campion, "A Review of Structure in the Selection Interview."

24. Paul F. Wernimont and John P. Campbell, "Signs, Samples, and Criteria," *Journal of Applied Psychology* 52, no. 5 (1968): 372–376.

25. Campion, Palmer, and Campion, "A Review of Structure in the Selection Interview."

26. Barrick, Swider, and Stewart, "Initial Evaluations in the Interview"; Barrick et al., "Candidate Characteristics Driving Initial Impressions during Rapport Building."

27. Mason and Schroeder, "Principal Hiring Practices."

28. Ibid.

29. Rutledge, Harris, Thompson, and Ingle, "Certify, Blink, Hire."

30. Scott A. Metzger and Meng-Jia Wu, "Commercial Teacher Selection Instruments: The Validity of Selecting Teachers Through Beliefs, Attitudes, and Values," *Review of Educational Research* 78, no. 4 (2008): 921–940.

31. Rutledge, Harris, Thompson, and Ingle, "Certify, Blink, Hire."

32. Ibid.

33. Campion, Palmer, and Campion, "A Review of Structure in the Selection Interview."

34. Ibid.

35. Ibid.

36. Ibid.

37. Ibid.

38. Ibid.

39. Ibid.

40. Allen I. Huffcutt and David J. Woehr, "Further Analysis of Employment Interview Validity: A Quantitative Evaluation of Interviewer-Related Structuring Methods," *Journal of Organizational Behavior* 20, no. 4 (1999): 549–560.

41. Ibid.

42. Campion, Palmer, and Campion, "A Review of Structure in the Selection Interview."

43. Ibid.

44. Ibid.

45. Philip L. Roth and James E. Campion, "An Analysis of the Predictive Power of the Panel Interview and Pre-Employment Tests," *Journal of Occupational and Organizational Psychology* 65, no. 1 (1992): 51–60; Huffcutt and Woehr, "Further Analysis of Employment Interview Validity"; McDaniel, Whetzel, Schmidt, and Maurer, "The Validity of Employment Interviews."

46. Mason and Schroeder, "Principal Hiring Practices."

47. Rutledge, Harris, Thompson, and Ingle, "Certify, Blink, Hire."

48. Campion, Palmer, and Campion, "A Review of Structure in the Selection Interview."

49. Ibid.

50. Huffcutt and Woehr, "Further Analysis of Employment Interview Validity."

51. Campion, Palmer, and Campion, "A Review of Structure in the Selection Interview."

52. Ibid.
53. Jennifer Hindman and James Stronge, "The $2 Million Decision: Teacher Selection and Principals' Interviewing Practices," *ERS Spectrum* 27, no. 3 (2009): 1–10.
54. Campion, Palmer, and Campion, "A Review of Structure in the Selection Interview."
55. Timothy Tran and Melinda C. Blackman, "The Dynamics and Validity of the Group Selection Interview," *Journal of Social Psychology* 146, no. 2 (2006): 183–201.
56. Louis A. Birenbaum, "Hiring for a Spa: Building a Team with Group Interviews," *Cornell Hotel and Restaurant Administration Quarterly* 30, no. 4 (1990): 53–56.
57. Gary C. Oliphant, Katharine Hansen, and Becky J. Oliphant, "A Review of a Telephone-Administered Behavior-Based Interview Technique," *Business Communication Quarterly* 71, no. 3 (2008): 383–386.
58. Annie Irvine, Paul Drew, and Roy Sainsbury, "'Am I Not Answering Your Questions Properly?' Clarification, Adequacy, and Responsiveness in Semi-Structured Telephone and Face-to-Face Interviews," *Qualitative Research* 13, no. 1 (2013): 87–106.
59. Susan G. Straus, Jeffrey A. Miles, and Laurie L. Levesque, "The Effects of Videoconference, Telephone, and Face-to-Face Media on Interviewer and Applicant Judgments in Employment Interviews," *Journal of Management* 27, no. 3 (2001): 363–381.
60. Talya N. Bauer et al., "Applicant Reactions to Different Selection Technology: Face-to-Face, Interactive Voice Response, and Computer-Assisted Telephone Screening Interviews," *International Journal of Selection and Assessment* 12, no. 1/2 (2004): 135–148.
61. Derek S. Chapman, Krista L. Uggerslev, and Jane Webster, "Applicant Reactions to Face-to-Face and Technology-Mediated Interviews: A Field Investigation," *Journal of Applied Psychology* 88, no. 5 (2003): 944–953.
62. Rutledge, Harris, Thompson, and Ingle, "Certify, Blink, Hire."
63. Barrick, Swider, and Stewart, "Initial Evaluations in the Interview."
64. Barrick et al., "Candidate Characteristics Driving Initial Impressions during Rapport Building."

Chapter 7
1. Paul F. Wernimont and John P. Campbell, "Signs, Samples, and Criteria," *Journal of Applied Psychology* 52, no. 5 (1968): 372–376.

2. Brian Rowan, Robin Jacob, and Richard Correnti, "Using Instructional Logs to Identify Quality in Educational Settings," *New Directions for Youth Development* 121, no. 8 (2009): 13–31.

3. Thomas Kersten, "Teacher Hiring Practices: Illinois Principals' Perspectives," *Educational Forum* 72, no. 4 (2008): 355–368; Richard W. Mason and Mark P. Schroeder, "Principal Hiring Practices: Toward a Reduction of Uncertainty," *The Clearing House* 83, no. 5 (2010): 186–193; Stacey A. Rutledge, Douglas N. Harris, Cynthia T. Thompson, and W. Kyle Ingle, "Certify, Blink, Hire: An Examination of the Process and Tools of Teacher Screening and Selection," *Leadership and Policy in Schools* 7, no. 3 (2008): 237–263.

4. Rutledge, Harris, Thompson, and Ingle, "Certify, Blink, Hire."

5. Daniel B. Felker, Patrick J. Curtin, and Andrew M. Rose, "Tests of Job Performance," in *Applied Measurement: Industrial Psychology in Human Resources Management*, ed. Deborah L. Whetzel and George R. Wheaton (Mahwah, NJ: Lawrence Erlbaum, 2007), 319–348.

6. Ibid.

7. Ibid.

8. Frank L. Schmidt and John E. Hunter, "The Validity and Utility of Selection Methods in Personnel Psychology: Practical and Theoretical Implications of 85 Years of Research Findings," *Psychological Bulletin* 124, no. 2 (1998): 262–274.

9. Mason and Schroeder, "Principal Hiring Practices."

10. Charles K. Parsons and Robert C. Liden, "Interviewer Perceptions of Applicant Qualifications: A Multivariate Field Study of Demographic Characteristics and Nonverbal Cues," *Journal of Applied Psychology* 69, no. 4 (1984): 557–568.

11. Ibid.

12. Timothy DeGroot and Stephan J. Motowidlo, "Visual and Vocal Interview Cues Can Affect Interviewers' Judgments and Predict Job Performance," *Journal of Applied Psychology* 84, no. 6 (1999): 986–993.

13. Jennifer R. Kogan et al., "Opening the Black Box of Clinical Skills Assessment via Observation: A Conceptual Model," *Medical Education* 45, no. 10 (2011): 1048–1060.

14. Anne H. Cash, Bridget K. Hamre, Robert C. Pianta, and Sonya S. Myers, "Rater Calibration When Observational Assessment Occurs at Large Scale: Degree of Calibration and Characteristics of Raters

Associated with Calibration," *Early Childhood Research Quarterly* 27, no. 3 (2012): 529–542.

15. American Educational Research Association (AERA), American Psychological Association (APA), and National Council on Measurement in Education (NCME), *Standards for Educational and Psychological Testing* (Washington, DC: AERA, 1999).

16. Cash, Hamre, Pianta, and Myers, "Rater Calibration When Observational Assessment Occurs at Large Scale"; Robert L. Johnson, James A. Penny, and Belita Gordon, *Assessing Performance: Designing, Scoring, and Validating Performance Tasks* (New York: Guilford Press, 2008).

17. Cash, Hamre, Pianta, and Myers, "Rater Calibration When Observational Assessment Occurs at Large Scale."

18. Michael A. Campion, David K. Palmer, and James E. Campion, "A Review of Structure in the Selection Interview," *Personnel Psychology* 50, no. 3 (1997): 655–702.

19. Heather C. Hill, Charlambos Y. Charalambous, and Matthew A. Kraft, "When Rater Reliability Is Not Enough: Teacher Observation Systems and a Case for the Generalizability Study," *Educational Researcher* 41, no. 2 (2012): 56–64.

20. Chad H. Van Iddekinge, Patrick H. Raymark, Philip L. Roth, and Holly S. Payne, "Comparing the Psychometric Characteristics of Ratings of Face-to-Face and Videotaped Structured Interviews," *International Journal of Selection and Assessment* 14, no. 4 (2006): 347–359.

21. Kogan et al., "Opening the Black Box of Clinical Skills Assessment via Observation."

22. Hill, Charalambous, and Kraft, "When Rater Reliability Is Not Enough."

23. Campion, Palmer, and Campion, "A Review of Structure in the Selection Interview"; Cash, Hamre, Pianta, and Myers, "Rater Calibration When Observational Assessment Occurs at Large Scale."

24. For example, see ibid; and Hill, Charalambous, and Kraft, "When Rater Reliability Is Not Enough."

25. David J. Woehr and Allen I. Huffcutt, "Rater Training for Performance Appraisal: A Quantitative Review," *Journal of Occupational and Organizational Psychology* 67, no. 3 (1994): 189–205.

26. Ibid.

27. Sylvia G. Roch and Brian J. O'Sullivan, "Frame of Reference Rater Training Issues: Recall, Time and Behavior Observation Training," *International Journal of Training and Development* 7, no. 2 (2003): 93–107.

28. Ibid.

Chapter 8

1. Equal Employment Opportunity Commission (EEOC), "Uniform Guidelines on Employee Selection Procedures (UGESP)," http://uniformguidelines.com/questionandanswers.html.
2. H. C. Taylor and J. T Russell, "The Relationship of Validity Coefficients to the Practical Effectiveness of Tests in Selection," *Journal of Applied Psychology* 23, no. 5 (1939): 565–578.
3. Wayne F. Cascio, Ralph A. Alexander, and Gerald V. Barrett, "Setting Cutoff Scores: Legal, Psychometric, and Professional Issues and Guidelines," *Personnel Psychology* 41, no. 1 (1988): 1–24.
4. Wayne F. Cascio and Herman Aguinis, "The Federal Uniform Guidelines on Employee Selection Procedures (1978): An Update on Selected Issues," *Review of Public Personnel Administration* 21, no. 3 (2001): 200–218.
5. Philip Bobko, Philip L. Roth, and Alan Nicewander, "Banding Selection Scores in Human Resource Management Decisions: Current Inaccuracies and the Effect of Conditional Standard Errors," *Organizational Research Methods* 8, no. 3 (2005): 259–273.

Chapter 9

1. Frank J. Landy and James L. Farr, *The Measurement of Work Performance: Methods, Theory, and Applications* (New York: Academic Press, 1983); William H. Bommer et al., "On the Interchangeability of Objective and Subjective Measures of Employee Performance: A Meta-Analysis," *Personnel Psychology* 48, no. 3 (1995): 588.
2. Landy and Farr, "Performance Rating"; William H. Bommer et al., "On the Interchangeability of Objective and Subjective Measures of Employee Performance."
3. Ibid.
4. Ibid.
5. John P. Campbell, "Modeling the Performance Prediction Problem in Industrial and Organizational Psychology," in *Handbook of Industrial and Organizational Psychology*, vol. 1, 2nd ed., ed. Marvin D. Dunnette and Leaetta M. Hough (Palo Alto, CA: Consulting Psychologists Press, 1990), 687–732; Jack M. Feldman, "Beyond Attribution Theory: Cognitive Processes in Performance Appraisal," *Journal of Applied Psychology* 66, no. 2 (1981): 127–148.

6. American Educational Research Association (AERA), American Psychological Association (APA), National Council on Measurement in Education (NCME), *Standards for Educational and Psychological Testing* (Washington, DC: AERA, 1999).

7. Kevin R. Murphy and Charles O. Davidshofer, *Psychological Testing: Principals and Applications,* 2nd ed. (Englewood Cliffs, NJ: Prentice-Hall, 1991), 80; J. C. Nunnally and I. H. Bernstein, *Psychometric Theory,* 3rd ed. (New York: McGraw-Hill, 1994).

8. Filip Lievens and Paul R. Sackett, "Situational Judgment Tests in High-Stakes Settings: Issues and Strategies with Generating Alternate Forms," *Journal of Applied Psychology* 92, no. 4 (2007): 1043–1055.

9. Paul R. Sackett, L. R. Burris, and Ann Marie Ryan, "Coaching and Practice Effects in Personnel Selection," in *International Review of Industrial and Organizational Psychology*, ed. Cary L. Cooper and Ivan T. Robertson (New York: Wiley, 2003), 145–183.

10. William T. Hoyt and Michael-David Kerns, "Magnitude and Moderators of Bias in Observer Ratings: A Meta-Analysis," *Psychological Methods* 4, no. 4 (1999): 403–424.

11. Ellen J. Langer, Susan Fiske, Shelley E. Taylor, and Benzion Chanowitz, "Stigma, Staring, and Discomfort: A Novel-Stimulus Hypothesis," *Journal of Experimental Social Psychology* 12, no. 5 (1976): 451–463.

12. William T. Hoyt and Michael-David Kerns, "Magnitude and Moderators of Bias in Observer Ratings: A Meta-Analysis," *Psychological Methods* 4, no. 4 (1999): 403–424.

13. Kevin R. Murphy and Jeanette N. Cleveland, *Understanding Performance Appraisal: Social, Organizational, and Goal-Based Perspectives* (Thousand Oaks, CA: Sage, 1995): 200.

14. Ibid.

15. Hoyt and Kerns, "Magnitude and Moderators of Bias in Observer Ratings."

16. David J. Woehr and Allen I. Huffcutt, "Rater Training for Performance Appraisal: A Quantitative Review," *Journal of Occupational and Organizational Psychology* 67, no. 3 (1994): 189–205.

17. Sylvia G. Roch, David J. Woehr, Vipanchi Mishra, and Urszula Kieszczynska, "Rater Training Revisited: An Updated Meta-Analytic Review of Frame-of-Reference Training," *Journal of Occupational and Organizational Psychology* 85, no. 3 (2012): 370–395.

18. Woehr and Huffcutt, "Rater Training for Performance Appraisal."

19. Roch, Woehr, Mishra, and Kieszczynska, "Rater Training Revisited."
20. H. John Bernardin and M. Ronald Buckley, "Strategies in Rater Training," *Academy of Management Review* 6, no. 2 (1981): 205–212.
21. Roch, Woehr, Mishra, and Kieszczynska, "Rater Training Revisited."
22. C. Allen Gorman and Joan R. Rentsch, "Evaluating Frame-of-Reference Rater Training Effectiveness Using Performance Schema Accuracy," *Journal of Applied Psychology* 94, no. 5 (2009): 1334–1344.
23. Michael A. Campion et al., "Doing Competencies Well: Best Practices in Competency Modeling," *Personnel Psychology* 64, no. 4 (2011): 225–262.
24. Ibid.
25. David Martone, "A Guide to Developing a Competency-Based Performance-Management System," *Employee Relations Today* 30, no. 3 (2003): 23–32.
26. Ibid.
27. Herbert G. Heneman III and Anthony T. Milanowski, "Assessing Human Resource Practices Alignment: A Case Study," *Human Resource Management* 50, no. 1 (2011): 45–64.
28. Campion et al., "Doing Competencies Well."
29. Heneman and Milanowski, "Assessing Human Resource Practices Alignment."
30. John P. Hausknecht, David V. Day, and Scott C. Thomas, "Applicant Reactions to Selection Procedures: An Updated Model and Meta-Analysis," *Personnel Psychology* 57, no. 3 (2004): 639–683.
31. Neil Anderson, Jesus F. Salgado, and Ute R. Hulsheger, "Applicant Reactions in Selection: Comprehensive Meta-Analysis into Reaction Generalization versus Situational Specificity," *International Journal of Selection and Assessment* 18, no. 3 (2010): 291–304.
32. Ibid.
33. Alan M. Saks and Krista L. Uggerslev, "Sequential and Combined Effects of Recruitment Information on Applicant Reactions," *Journal of Business Psychology* 25, no. 3 (2010): 351–365.
34. Sonja Schinkel, Annelies van Vianen, and Dirk van Dierendonck, "Selection Fairness and Outcomes: A Field Study of Interactive Effects on Applicant Reactions," *International Journal of Selection and Assessment* 21, no. 1 (2013): 22–31.
35. Brad A. Chambers, "Applicant Reaction and Their Consequences: Review, Advice, and Recommendations for Future Research," *International Journal of Management Reviews* 4, no. 4 (2002): 317–333.

36. AERA, APA, NCME, *Standards for Educational and Psychological Testing.*
37. Robert M. Guion, "Criterion Measurement and Personnel Judgments," *Personnel Psychology* 14, no. 2 (1961): 141–149.
38. Ibid.
39. Bommer et al., "On the Interchangeability of Objective and Subjective Measures of Employee Performance."
40. Walter C. Borman and Stephan J. Motowidlo, "Task Performance and Contextual Performance: The Meaning for Personnel Selection Research," *Human Performance* 10, no. 2 (1997): 99–109.
41. Ibid.
42. Ibid.
43. Wayne F. Cascio and Herman Aguinis, *Applied Psychology in Human Resource Management,* 7th ed. (New York: Prentice Hall, 2011), 63–65.
44. Guion, "Criterion Measurement and Personnel Judgments."
45. Maury A. Buster, Philip L. Roth, and Philip Bobko, "A Process for Content Validation of Education and Experience-Based Minimum Qualifications: An Approach Resulting in Federal Court Approval," *Personnel Psychology* 58, no. 3 (2005): 771–799.
46. Congress of the United States Office of Technology Assessment, *The Use of Integrity Tests for Pre-Employment Screening OTA-SET-442* (Washington, DC: Government Printing Office, 1990), 32.
47. Michael A. Campion, David K. Palmer, and James E. Campion, "A Review of Structure in the Selection Interview," *Personnel Psychology* 50, no. 3 (1997): 655–702.
48. David E. Terpstra and R. Bryan Kethley, "Organizations' Relative Degree of Exposure to Selection Discrimination Litigation," *Public Personnel Management* 31, no. 3 (2002): 277–292.
49. Ibid.
50. Ibid.
51. Ibid.
52. Dale S. Rose, *The Relationship Between Sample Size and Measurement Reliability as Applied to Banding in Continuous Hiring Settings* Ann Arbor, MI: University Microfilms, 1997 (UMI No. 9734229).
53. Michael A. Campion et al., "The Controversy Over Score Banding in Personnel Selection: Answers to 10 Key Questions," *Personnel Psychology* 54, no. 1 (2001): 150.

ACKNOWLEDGMENTS

I thank the best of my many teachers—and the people who hired them. This book would not be what it is without each of my teacher's courage and skill in showing me how to be a better thinker, writer, and researcher. Specifically, these include Jean Keniston, Tom Rose, Michaela Parks, Erwin Gruenebaum, John Graham, Neal Stumbo, Olivia Carter, Jack Mingo, Mr. Alden, Gretchen Griswold, Stan Cardinet, Mike Golston, Kathleen Aldrich-Wolfe, Dave Kinstle, David Harrington, Elliot Aronson, Arthur Aron, Elaine Aron, Jane Halpert, Ramzi Baydoun, Stephen Steinhaus, and David Nygren. I also thank my daughter, Isabella, for the inspiration to write this book. I hope that she and others in her generation will continue to enjoy learning—even in school.

Dale S. Rose

When I think of an excellent teacher, Bill Hopkins leaps to the front of my mind. His guidance and patience with this overinquisitive undergrad will always be humbly appreciated. I thank my parents, David and Susan English, for providing my education and making sacrifices to ensure I attended high-quality schools early on. I also thank all of my family, yes, you Mimi,

253

Kiersten, Charlotte, and DC. I hope we see these methods in practice as you begin your formal education. Last but not least, to my wife, Hava Liberman, thanks for being supportive and simply for being you.

Andrew English

To my husband, Zach, a brilliant teacher and researcher and the love of my life—thank you for believing in me. I thank my daughters, Elizabeth and Caitlin, who find joy in the little things. I am grateful to my parents, Sid Gillespie and the late Polly Whitmire, who encouraged me to dream beyond the boundaries that were set by others and who instilled in me a love of learning. My appreciation extends to my brother, Justin Gillespie, whose determination inspires others. And I especially recognize the teachers who shaped my thinking and significantly influenced my career choices, especially Fred Switzer, Alice Stuhlmacher, and Jane Halpert.

Treena Gillespie Finney

ABOUT THE AUTHORS

Dale S. Rose is the president of 3D Group, a California-based consulting firm specializing in human resources assessment and development. He is an expert in measurement, leadership development, program evaluation, and employee surveys. Rose has authored more than a dozen commercial assessments for identifying and developing talent. Before founding 3D Group, he developed and validated many widely used selection systems for Ameritech and a test publishing subsidiary of National Computer Systems (NCS). While at Ameritech, he built and validated the Engineering Clerk Test, which was used for over a decade to screen employees in nearly every technical job at the company. While at NCS, he built and validated the Management Aptitude Test, the Customer Service Index, and dozens of customized hiring systems for Fortune 500 companies. Since founding 3D Group, Rose has applied his measurement talents to many educational institutions, including charter schools such as KIPP, Uplift Education, and Idea Academy. He also works in higher education, evaluating programs such as the Stanford Educational Leadership Institute and the Wharton School Leadership Program for the Girl Scouts. He consults regularly for foundations and nonprofit and public agencies such as the Bill & Melinda Gates Foundation, Reading in Motion, Stagebridge, and the California Department of Education.

Rose earned his doctoral degree in industrial and organizational psychology from DePaul University, with a minor in organizational effectiveness technologies. In addition to his consulting and academic pursuits, he is the president of the board at Maybeck High School, a small private high school in Berkeley, California.

Andrew English is a senior consultant at 3D Group, a California-based consulting firm specializing in assessment of human resources. He has expertise in the implementation of 360-degree feedback programs, employee surveys, psychometrics, team consultation, and leadership coaching. English has coached clients across a wide range of industries, including technology/software, education, pharmaceuticals, government, and service. His personal management experience ranges from working as a mental health counselor and statistician for a nonprofit child abuse prevention center to working at one of the largest defense industry contractors in the United States. As the executive director for a nonprofit organization, he managed a team of staff and contractors that provided finance consulting and training for the finance industry. In both his work heading up a virtual team research lab and working as a research consultant for ThoughtLink, he studied how virtual teams perform effectively. English has authored several assessments for identifying and developing talent, and in the past five years he has worked with several nationally recognized charter schools to help them build better personnel selection systems and leadership development programs. He also taught at Florida Institute of Technology

(FIT), where he supervised the 3T Research Group (Teams, Training, and Technology). In addition to teaching other psychology courses, he taught research methods for several years. He continues to publish and present research on team measurement issues, individual assessment, and 360-degree feedback.

English earned his doctorate in industrial organizational psychology from FIT. He has MSs in industrial organizational psychology and clinical psychology from FIT and a bachelor's degree from Auburn University in psychology. He is a member of the Society of Industrial Organizational Psychology and the American Psychological Association.

Treena Gillespie Finney is an associate professor of management at the University of South Alabama, where she teaches human resource management and organizational behavior courses at the undergraduate and graduate levels. Treena's research interests focus on performance management, particularly improving management competencies through the use of effective appraisal and feedback. Her other research interests include employee perceptions of fairness, selection issues, and the application of human resource practices cross-culturally. Her work has appeared in such refereed journals as the *Journal of Business and Psychology, Organizational Behavior and Human Decision Processes,* and *Journal of Management Education.* Prior to entering academia, Finney led human resources research projects for Disneyland Resort in Anaheim, California, and worked in organizational effectiveness for United Airlines, where she developed employee selection systems for customer-contact groups and managed corporate projects, such as 360-degree feedback and performance evaluation. She continues to work on consulting projects related to employee selection and performance appraisal, providing consulting services to public-sector and private-sector organizations.

Finney earned her doctorate in industrial and organizational psychology from DePaul University and her MS in applied psychology and BA in psychology, with a minor in marketing, from Clemson University. She is a member of the Academy of Management, the Society for Industrial/Organizational Psychology, and the Society for Human Resource Management.

INDEX

job-related interviews, 104
job simulations, 60–61, 68

knowledge
    declarative, 92
    procedural, 92
knowledge, skills, abilities, and other
    characteristics (KSAOs), 30–33,
    35–39, 41, 98, 100, 110–112, 162,
    188–189, 201–202, 216

letters of reference, 77
low-fidelity simulations, 91–92

math teachers, 10
measurement error, 44–45
minimum cutoff approach, 161–162
motor skills work samples, 88–89
multicultural attitudes, 80
multiple cutoff approach, 160–164
multiple interviewers, 122–126

negative correlation, 53–54
nonverbal cues, 140–141
note-taking, during interviews, 120–
    121, 132

objectivity, 172–177
online application forms, 75–76
opportunity costs, 157
organizational fit, 39–41, 80–81

panel interviews, 59–60, 122–126
pass rate, 155–156

performance criteria, 197–201
performance dimension training, 146
performance measures, 172–177
personal qualities, 26–28, 62, 112–113,
    131, 139–140
person-job (PJ) fit, 39–41
person-organization (PO) fit, 39–41,
    80–81
phone interviews, 68, 128–130
poor performing teachers, firing of,
    21–22
portfolios, 92–93
predictive study, 202–203
prequalified candidates, 221–222
principals
    on demonstration videos, 138–139
    hiring decisions by, 4–6, 12, 28–29,
        67–69, 212–213
    interviews by, 112–113, 126, 131
    resistance by, to selection tools,
        212–213
    views on teacher effectiveness, 27–29
probationary periods, 12–13, 87
procedural knowledge, 92
professional communication, 97
professional development, 14, 20–21
professional qualifications, 26–28, 61–
    62, 113, 139
psychological interviews, 59, 104–105
psychomotor work samples, 89–90

racial diversity, 29
random error, 47, 74
rater training, 145–147, 184–186
rating rubrics
    interpretations of, 183
    for interviews, 119–120, 131–135
recruiting pool base rate of success,
    158–160

262